Free to Choose

DAVE McCASLAND

This book is designed for your personal reading pleasure and profit. It is also designed for group study. A leader's guide with visual aids (SonPower Multiuse Transparency Masters), and Rip-Offs (student activity booklets) are available from your local Christian bookstore or from the publisher.

BOOKS a division of SP Publications, Inc.
WHEATON, ILLINOIS 60187

Offices also in
Whitby, Ontario, Canada
Amersham-on-the-Hill, Bucks, England

Second printing, 1984

All Bible quotations, unless otherwise indicated, are from the *New International Version,* © 1978 by the New York International Bible Society. Used by permission. Other quotations are from the *King James Version* (KJV) and from the *New Testament in Modern English* (Phillips) (PH), © 1959 by J. B. Phillips.

Library of Congress Catalog Number: 83-60820
ISBN: 0-88207-593-4

Recommended Dewey Decimal Classification: 248.83
Suggested Subject Headings: YOUTH—RELIGIOUS LIFE: BIBLE. O.T. BIOGRAPHY

© 1983, Dave McCasland. All rights reserved.
Printed in the United States of America.

VICTOR BOOKS
A division of SP Publications, Inc.
Wheaton, Ill. 60187

Dedication

*To Bob and Evon Potter,
who put up with our
loud cars and our late nights,
to help us find Christ.*

Contents

1. A Life That Counts **9**
   choosing a foundation for living (Genesis 37—50)
2. I Didn't Ask for This Family **18**
   choosing your own direction (37:1-4)
3. All You Can Be **26**
   choosing to dream big (37:5-11)
4. When the Bottom Falls Out **37**
   choosing to stick with God (37:12-36)
5. The Key to Opportunity **49**
   choosing to serve (39:1-6)
6. Life Without Walls **60**
   choosing what you really want (39:6-23)
7. Being Good, for Nothing? **69**
   choosing to trust in the dark (39:11-21)
8. On Top of the Bottom **79**
   choosing to help others (39:21—40:8)
9. Let Down Again **89**
   choosing to keep on trying (40:9-23)
10. How to Handle Success **101**
    choosing to be humble (41:1-57)
11. Getting Rid of the Garbage **113**
    choosing to forgive (42—44)
12. Why, God? **125**
    choosing to accept God's sovereignty (45:1-28)
13. Turning Trash into Treasure **136**
    choosing to see the big picture (50:15-21)

A Life That Counts
1

Genesis 37—50

At the age of 17, Joseph had it made. He was a good-looking guy with a great build, the favorite son of a wealthy father. His future seemed to hold nothing but rainbows.

But then the bottom fell out. Just when it seemed that Joseph was ready to fly, his life crash-landed. For the next 13 years, he was "dumped on" by nearly everyone he knew.

• His own brothers—who hated him—plotted to kill him, but decided to sell him into slavery instead.

• He was falsely accused of rape by the wife of his employer and sent to prison.

• He was put in charge of the prison, where the warden took credit for all of Joseph's hard work.

• He helped a fellow prisoner gain release, and the prisoner promised to return the favor when he got out. The man forgot.

Joseph could have responded to his problems in a number of different ways:

(1) He could have become a chronic complainer.

(2) He could have decided that life was the pits, and killed himself.

(3) He could have tossed out his faith in God and decided that if life was so crazy and unjust, the only solution was to live for himself.

Joseph could have responded in any of those ways, and who could have blamed him? But he didn't. Instead Joseph chose to trust God and stick with Him even when it seemed that everything in his life was out of control.

Where Do You Build a Life?

I believe the key to understanding Joseph's reaction to misfortune and injustice is to examine the *foundation* of his life. We have the advantage of seeing Joseph's life from beginning to end in the Book of Genesis, and here's what it shows us:

Joseph committed his life to God when he was young, and he never backed out of that commitment. Joseph built his life on faith in the living God, and his foundation endured the most intense pressure.

During the 1930s, the city of Denver decided to build a dam in the high country of the Colorado Rockies. The reservoir created by this dam was to hold back the rushing waters of Lost Creek and help provide water for the city.

For months workmen built roads into the area and then brought in equipment to begin

A Life That Counts / 11

construction of the dam. In a beautiful little aspen grove, some log cabins were constructed for the people living and working at the project site.

Finally the workmen began pouring the concrete for the foundation of the dam. They poured and poured, but the concrete just seemed to disappear down the shaft they had dug. Then someone discovered that instead of pouring the concrete onto solid bedrock, they were pouring onto a layer of decomposed granite. The gravel-like rock had given way, and the concrete was being swallowed up in the heart of the mountain as fast as it could be poured in. Hundreds of thousands of dollars and tons of concrete later, the project was abandoned.

Today you can backpack into that same area, but you won't find a dam. Traces of the road are still visible, and if you look closely into the underbrush, you'll see the rusted hulk of a car or truck. The shells of the log cabins are still there, and the "shaft house" covers the hole into which the concrete was poured. It stands as a silent reminder to the futility of trying to build without bedrock.

You can't build a dam, a house, or a life without a solid foundation. The principle is stated so plainly in the Bible:

> Unless the Lord builds the house,
> its builders labor in vain.
> Unless the Lord watches over the city,
> the watchmen stand guard in vain
> (Psalm 127:1).

That's one reason why making a personal commitment to Jesus Christ is so important. To accept Christ as your Saviour and Lord is to choose a solid foundation on which the rest of your life will be built.

Maybe you've sung the hymn, "On Christ the solid rock I stand; all other ground is sinking sand." What does that mean to you? To me it means that Christ is the only safe foundation on which to build a life.

Remember the parable Jesus told about the wise and foolish builders? One man built his house on the rock; the other man built on the sand. The rain came, the streams rose, and the winds blew and beat against both houses. One house stood and the other one fell.

Jesus' observation was, "Everyone who hears these words of Mine and puts them into practice is like a wise man who built his house on the rock. . . . But everyone who hears these words of Mine and does not put them into practice is like a foolish man who built his house on sand" (Matthew 7:24, 26).

Sand-y Excuses

At this point, let's ask an obvious question: Why would anyone build a house on sand? Anyone with half a brain would know better. Or would he? Keep in mind Jesus' comparison between building a house and building a life. Then consider the following possible excuses for "building on sand."

(1) "I don't plan to live here all my life. I'm young, and what I'm doing now is just temporary, kind of an experiment. Youth is the time to try all kinds of things. When I get older, I plan to move into a more permanent house built on a rock somewhere."

(2) "Everyone else is building around here, so

it must be a good place. Surely all these other people can't be mistaken about the location."

(3) "I think the storm problem is overrated. When people get older, they worry about things like storms. But right now, well, I can't spend much time thinking about something that may never happen."

(4) "It's easier to build on sand. Building on rock takes a lot of work."

The problem with building on sand is that if a person tries to build a life on any foundation other than Jesus Christ, somewhere down the line the very basis of that life is going to shift and cause problems.

A friend of mine has a big problem—his backyard keeps disappearing. The housing division where he lives is built in an old coal mining area. The ground beneath the houses is honeycombed with air shafts from the abandoned mines. From time to time in my friend's backyard, a six-foot circle of earth falls in. Now he's wondering when his house will go!

Why all the fuss about foundations? Because you can't build a solid life on a shaky base. Every life has a foundation, and no one can choose yours except you.

How Do You Spell Success?

In this book we're going to examine the life of a young man who weathered some nasty storms. He came out all right, but not because he was lucky or because God liked him more than other people. Joseph was successful because of his foundation for living, and because his foundation determined his *attitudes* and *choices*.

Evidently, early in his life, Joseph decided he was going to live for God. No matter where it took him, no matter what it cost him, no matter what anyone else did, he was going to live for Almighty God.

He had many opportunities to change his mind, but he never did. Even when his decisions to remain faithful to God resulted in hardship, he stayed true to the Lord. He chose a solid foundation for his life and stuck to it. His basic commitment influenced every decision he made.

Not far from me lives an attractive young lady who never had a date till she was a senior in high school. It wasn't because she didn't want to date or was never asked—she simply didn't have time.

For years she got up at 3 A.M., seven days a week, in order to get ice time at the Broadmoor World Arena. Her goal was to be a figure skater, and her dedication was part of the price she had to pay. Every decision of her life was made on the basis of how it affected her ice skating.

Figure skating determined where she went, what she ate, how she exercised, when she went to school, who her friends were—everything!

Joseph's life teaches us that if we want to be followers of God, we must begin with a basic commitment to Him and make every other decision in light of that commitment.

Some people think that having Christ in their life is like having little brother with them on a date—it takes away the fun and excitement. On the contrary, life with Christ is an adventure. It's an experience that calls for everything we have and gives back more than we can ever imagine. But we have to *choose* it.

Choose Your Attitude

A book and a job have greatly affected my outlook on life. The book, *Man's Search For Meaning*, was written by Viktor Frankl. Dr. Frankl is an Austrian psychiatrist who was imprisoned by the Nazis during World War II.

In the concentration camp he literally lost everything he had. His father, mother, brother, and wife all died in the camps or the gas chambers. Frankl and his sister were the only members of his entire family who survived.

All his possessions were taken from him, as well as his identity and status as a doctor. He was reduced to doing manual labor and fighting to stay alive in the camp. In a sense, he was even stripped of his human dignity.

Yet Dr. Frankl found that there was one thing that could not be taken from him. He concluded that when everything else is gone, the one thing that remains is "the last of the human freedoms—the ability to choose one's attitude in a given set of circumstances" (*Man's Search For Meaning*, Washington Square Press, p. 104). Dr. Frankl not only survived the concentration camp, but profited from the experience because of the attitude he chose.

How many times have you heard someone say, "I had to do it. I had no choice"? According to Frankl, the one thing we always have is a choice, even if only the choice of what our attitude will be.

The other tremendous influence on my life was a job I had working on a guest ranch in the Colorado mountains. It had affected my attitude and outlook, perhaps more than anything else in my life. Every summer break, I would escape the Oklahoma heat by heading for the Rockies.

It was, in one sense, a dream job for a college student. I had the opportunity to be on my own, learn some new things, and receive spiritual input from a Christian man I greatly respected. But it was also the hardest job I ever had.

We often joked, "We only work half a day here—12 hours." It was usually more like 14 or 16 hours. The work that needed to be done was always being interrupted by work that *had* to **be** done, like when a cloudburst filled the boiler room with gravel, or when a truck broke down and had to be repaired. Then after a full day of work there were evening programs to be given for the guests.

Time after time the ranch manager challenged us with these words, "Your attitude can change any situation." I learned that sometimes I couldn't directly change the situation, but I could always change my attitude. And when I changed my attitude, it changed me—my approach, my effort, my ability to think clearly and calmly, my courage and willingness to try when the situation appeared hopeless.

Choose to Learn, Learn to Choose

If it has been a while since you've examined the life of Joseph, why not set aside some time to read Genesis 37—50. As you study his life, I think you will encounter, time and again, these two truths:

(1) *You always have the freedom to choose your attitude in any set of circumstances.*

(2) *Your attitude can change any situation.*

Joseph made some amazing choices in light of his difficult circumstances. He maintained a positive attitude when most other people would have screamed, "What's the use!" He did it, not because he was superhuman, but because he had chosen God's path in life and God was with him.

Where do you stand on your most important choice in life? Is Jesus Christ the Lord of your life? Have you committed yourself to Him, trusting Him for forgiveness of your sins? Have you decided to follow Him, to be His, whatever it costs?

Your choice determines the foundation on which your life will be built. It's a decision that only you can make. When that issue is settled, you can begin to deal with the attitudes and choices that affect the direction of your life each day.

Is there anything in Joseph's life that might be a help to you? There is if you face conflicts in your family from time to time; or wonder about what you're going to do in life; or think about finding someone who really loves you; or need to know how to handle people who make life miserable for you.

Joseph's life says to each of us, "You always have a choice. With God's help, you can choose the best."

I Didn't Ask for This Family 2

Genesis 37:1-4

Families are like noses in a lot of ways.
   Everybody has one.
   They are all different.
   They are issued, not selected.
   They are easily damaged in fights, often bleed, and sometimes break.
   We usually think that others' are better than ours.
   Noses and families—things about which we have little or no choice. Or have we?
   Though we can't choose our families, we *can* choose how we live with them. In chapter 1 we saw that we are free to choose our attitude in any given situation. Our family relationships are a good place to start.

I Didn't Ask for This Family / 19

Family Feuds

There are few really "good" families mentioned in the Bible. On a scale of one to ten, I would rate most of them about a five, with many down around a one or two.

Take Cain and Abel, for example. In the world's first family, one brother killed the other (Genesis 4:1-12).

Or how about Samuel? Instead of being raised by his natural parents, he grew up under Eli as an apprentice priest. Eli's sons were juvenile delinquents who became two of the worst adults in the whole country (1 Samuel 1:1—2:26).

Moses grew up as a member of a racial minority who was adopted into a royal family. He may have gone to school with the other royal kids, but he and everyone else knew he was different (Exodus 2:1-10).

When you look at the biblical characters who achieved greatness, most of them came from less than ideal family situations. They were not successful because they had all the advantages; they were successful because they overcame their disadvantages.

The same is true of Joseph. You can't say he was successful because he came from a model family. Take a closer look at his situation.

Joseph lived in a "blended" family. He and his 11 brothers were all sons of Jacob, but they had four different mothers. Can you imagine the conflict and competition in that household? And we think the problems of today's step-families, created by death, divorce, and remarriage, are something new! Joseph knew all about living with stepbrothers.

Joseph's father loved Joseph more than he loved his other sons. Rachel had been Jacob's favorite wife, and he loved her children, Joseph and Benjamin, more than the others. It wasn't fair, but that's how it was.

You might think Jacob's partiality would put Joseph in the driver's seat. But favoritism has damaging effects in any situation—especially within a family. Think how students feel about a "teacher's pet" who gets higher grades than others who produce better work; or a coach's klutzy son who starts the game; or the girl who gets all kinds of honors just because she's pretty. And how do you feel about someone in your own family who seems to get more privileges than you?

Joseph's brothers hated him. Joseph wasn't discriminated against; he was discriminated *toward.* That made his relationship with his brothers even tougher. The fact that Joseph was next to the youngest and had special privileges didn't help matters.

Home Improvements

Why spend all these words discussing what a horrible family life Joseph had? First, it might help you realize that things aren't so bad at your house. Even if your family isn't perfect, it probably isn't as bad as Joseph's.

A second reason for taking a close look at Joseph's family is just in case things *are* as bad for you as they were for him, or even if they're worse. You can gain a lot of encouragement by seeing how Joseph overcame the obstacles of a difficult family experience.

Not long ago, Dr. Blair Justice and his wife spent several months studying the characteristics of healthy or "successful" families. One of the Justices' conclusions was that successful families are not those without problems, but those who are learning how to solve the problems they have. The "successful" families they described were coping with death, divorce, alcoholism, and runaway teens.

Those families were coping because someone in each family had taken the risk of opening up, sharing, and listening to the feelings of the others. Someone had decided to choose a new direction, a better way. And that choice made a difference in the entire family.

What can you do to overcome the problems in your family?

Peacemaking

First, *do everything you can to live at peace with the rest of your family.* If your home situation is like some, you may think this suggestion sounds like telling sheep to go live in peace with the wolves. But peacemaking is God's command and plan for each of us.

"Do not repay anyone evil for evil. Be careful to do what is right in the eyes of everybody. If it is possible, as far as it depends on you, live at peace with everyone" (Romans 12:17-18).

I like to remember things by using alliteration. So if I wanted to learn Romans 12:17-18, my alliterative translation would be: "Peacemaking precludes pernicious pronouncements while placing priority on patience and persistence." (You possibly prefer the proper, precise translation, prohibiting paraphrases.) In other words, we have to watch what we do and keep working for harmony in the family even after everyone else has given up.

"A gentle answer turns away wrath, but a harsh word stirs up anger" (Proverbs 15:1). Store that in your mental computer, and see how it affects the way you talk to the people you live with. The greatest silencer in the world is a gentle answer. Peace in the home often begins when we decide to watch what we say.

The Apostle Peter, who in his younger days had often put his sandal in his mouth, wrote: "Whoever would love life and see good days must keep his tongue from evil and his lips from deceitful speech. He must turn from evil and do good; he must seek peace and pursue it" (1 Peter 3:10-11).

Why should we "seek peace and pursue it"? Because peace comes only when someone is willing to keep on trying. When everyone gives up, it's all over.

Communication

A second thing you can do about family problems is *learn effective ways to communicate.*

A psychiatrist recently noted that sexual attraction is rarely the main reason why teenage girls get pregnant before marriage. But sex is one way teens communicate the rebellion they feel toward their parents. Running away from home, experimenting with alcohol and drugs, deliberately failing in school, and defying parental values are other ways of making a statement:

"You don't act like you love me."
"I hate it that you're getting divorced."
"Nobody cares what I think around here."
"I have a mind. I can think for myself."

The value of learning effective ways to communicate is that we can express ourselves with well-chosen words instead of destructive actions.

Parents may also lack communication skills. They sometimes fail to talk, listen, and try to understand their children's viewpoints. Parents too may still be learning how to communicate, and they need their children's help and patience.

On Your Own?

Finally, you can *decide to follow Christ with all your heart*. It's your choice, no matter what your friends or family decide. You are responsible to set the direction of your life.

Following the correct course of action may not solve all the problems in your family. It didn't for Joseph. Even though he was a young man with deep faith in God, it didn't stop his brothers' hatred or reverse his father's favoritism. But it did keep Joseph from letting his rotten family situation ruin his life.

He was willing to take the right direction even when others in his family weren't. He became a stronger person because of his choice to follow the Lord—even if it meant going it alone.

It was Abraham Lincoln who said: "I don't know who my grandfather was; I am much more concerned to know what his grandson will be."

We don't get to choose our families, but we *do* have a choice about how we live with them.

Before You Read On

In each chapter of this book you will find, as in this chapter, some suggestions to help you apply biblical truths to your own experiences. One of the most exciting things about being a Christian is discovering God's direction through His Word.

As a high school sophomore, I was invited to attend a Saturday night Bible study. When I got there I discovered some remarkable people. They were all students my own age who kept talking about what they were "getting from the Word." I had owned a Bible all my life, but had never "gotten" a thing from it.

When those students shared the results of their Bible study, they kept saying things like, "God spoke to me from Psalm 23" or "The Lord is leading me to do this or that." The teachings they studied in the Bible actually affected the way they lived and the choices they made.

I was impressed, but mystified. Did they hear voices? Did they have to study a long time before God "spoke" to them? How could I get in on this "being led" business?

For months I attended the group, completed my Bible studies, and began memorizing Scripture. The first noticeable result was an awareness that I needed to make Jesus Christ the Lord of my life. I realized that He wanted to lead me, but first I had to place myself in His hands by faith, and agree to go His way.

I Didn't Ask for This Family / 25

Then one afternoon not long after committing my life to Christ, I was driving and listening to my car radio. It was playing a song about a "calendar girl." My brain was following a predictable series of mental images "starring" one of those well-put-together models that pose for calendar pictures. Then a verse of Scripture came to mind:

"Whatsoever things are true ... honest ... just ... pure ... lovely ... of good report ... think on these things" (Philippians 4:8, KJV).

It occurred to me that there were better things to think about than the images conjured up by the words of that song. I switched off the radio and began moving in a different mental direction.

Suddenly it hit me! That was it! That was what all my friends had been talking about. God had spoken to me from His Word and it had affected my behavior. There was no voice from the sky or spooky experience. Yet God had come into my daily life in a very real way. He had made me aware of a better alternative which He wanted me to choose. It was so simple, yet so profound.

Hopefully, this book will help you move toward discovering God's leading in your own life. That's the reason for the practical suggestions you'll find throughout. They aren't intended to be preachy paragraphs, but practical pointers to help you apply the Bible's truth to your everyday life.

All You Can Be
3

Genesis 37:5-11

If you were to drop by my house early one morning, you might find my family at the breakfast table describing their dreams from the night before. Sometimes it's a weird way to start the day.

Dreams have fascinated people for centuries. In Old Testament days, dreams were taken very seriously as messages from God and predictions of events. The Bible states plainly that many times God used dreams to communicate with a variety of people. A person who could interpret dreams was held in high regard as we'll see later in Joseph's life.

Dream On

Today the word *dream* is used in many different ways. It is often used to describe the activity of our minds when we are asleep.

Dream can also refer to a wish or desire. Sometimes it's a wild fantasy with no connection to reality. In other cases, it may be possible, but highly unlikely. It might center around thoughts of great achievement or a desire to change one's physical appearance. Whatever form it takes, this type of dream remains only a wish—an unattainable goal that stays in the mind and out of reach.

But dreams can be more than nighttime images or far-out thoughts during history class. A *dream* can also be an ambition related to a goal toward which you are working. As someone expressed it, "No dream comes true until you wake up and go to work." Such a dream has its own built-in motivation. It inspires effort and dedication.

Martin Luther King, Jr. will be remembered for his leadership in the struggle for racial equality. During a civil rights march on Washington in 1963, he stood at the Lincoln Memorial and addressed 200,000 persons, while millions of others watched on television.

In his stirring speech, King said: "I have a dream that one day this nation will rise up and live out the true meaning of its creed: 'We hold these truths to be self-evident; that all men are created equal.' " Dr. King had a *dream*. To some it seemed like a wild fantasy, but he gave his life to turning that dream into reality.

Yosuf Karsh has photographed many of the world's great people. Winston Churchill, Albert Einstein, Ernest Hemingway, and many others have been uniquely recorded through Karsh's camera lens. In his photography, Karsh tries to capture the inner power of people who have left their marks on society.

"I have found that great people do have some things in common," says Karsh. "One is an immense belief in themselves and in their mission. They also have great determination as well as an ability to work hard" (*Parade*, December 3, 1978).

If you want to accomplish something important in life, you have to begin with a goal and a sense of mission. You have to have a dream.

But dreaming is not without its problems. A person who is pursuing a dream and going somewhere in life is often resented by others. When Joseph had a dream and told his brothers, they hated him even more (Genesis 37:5-11). In one sense, it's easy to see why.

Joseph's brothers understood his dream to mean that one day he would rule over them. In Old Testament times, the oldest son was always first in line for the inheritance of material goods and authority. Everyone else lined up behind him in order of age. Joseph was number 11 in a family of 12. And there he was telling his 10 older brothers that one day they would be bowing down to him. Obviously, they weren't thrilled.

When Joseph shared his second dream, even his father got upset (Genesis 37:9-11). As much as Jacob loved Joseph, this second dream was a bit too much. Circumstances later proved that Joseph was right in *what* he said about his dreams. But he was probably wrong in *how* he said it.

The Pride Trap

One of the dangers in dreaming big is that the dreamer can develop a superior attitude.

Christians need to be aware of this danger. Even if someone gives us a hard time about our Christian convictions, it doesn't give us the right to take an "I'm right, you're wrong" approach.

When the Apostle Peter gave instructions to Christians on how to witness he warned: "But in your hearts set apart Christ as Lord. Always be prepared to give an answer to everyone who asks you to give the reason for the hope that you have. But do this with gentleness and respect, keeping a clear conscience, so that those who speak maliciously against your good behavior in Christ may be ashamed of their slander" (1 Peter 3:15-16).

As Christians, we should always answer others respectfully and share our faith with gentleness. We aren't given a license to clobber others with spiritual truth in a superior manner.

Perhaps Joseph was just naive when he told his dreams to his family. Or maybe he was full of pride. Whatever his motive, his dreams annoyed his brothers and intensified the jealousy they already felt toward him.

On the other hand, Jacob must have known there was some truth to the dreams. After rebuking Joseph, "His father kept the thing in mind" (Genesis 37:11).

Lonely Dreamers

Another drawback to pursuing a dream is that the dreamer must face frequent periods of loneliness. Many high school students have narrow limits for accepting others. If you go along with the crowd on most things and don't rock the boat, you'll fit in OK. But what if your priorities aren't the same as most other people your age? What if you take the Bible seriously and want your life to count for Jesus Christ?

Faith doesn't have to brand you as some kind of freak, but it may cause conflicts over certain issues. Sometimes your "dream"—to live a life that counts for Christ—can leave you sitting home alone.

In Yosuf Karsh's description of his famous photo subjects, the noted photographer said: "I've also seen that great men are often lonely. This is understandable, because they have built such high standards for themselves that they often feel alone. But that same loneliness is part of their ability to create. Character, like a photograph, develops in darkness" (*Parade*).

I'm not very good at standing alone, but I'm learning more about it as I go through life. One time, I was shamed into realizing how far off the mark I had gotten.

During high school and college, I did what I considered "more than my share" of standing alone for my Christian faith. It eventually became little more than something I did out of obligation. I was tired of being a social leper.

So when I entered the army, I decided to put my faith in my footlocker and be "one of the boys." It was easier than I thought. No one around me cared whether I was a Christian or not.

But something about one guy in our basic training platoon bothered me. He was different, but I couldn't quite figure out why.

He was quiet, never yelled or swore, and didn't seem to have the same priorities as most soldiers.

Besides that, he always waited to be the last man in the shower. And when he finally got there, he mumbled to himself the whole time. One night I decided to confront him.

"Robinson," I said. "Why do you always shower last and talk to yourself?"

He smiled and identified himself as a member of a religious group I had always considered "off the wall." "I spent two years in Japan as a missionary," he said, "so while I'm showering I pray in Japanese. It gives me a few quiet minutes at the end of the day, and helps me stay fresh in the language."

I didn't tell him anything about my "faith," or rather lack of it at that point. But I have never forgotten his willingness, in an uncomfortable situation, to stand alone for what he believed. If you're going to walk God's path in life, and dream big for Him, you'd better expect some rocky places.

Dreams That Come True

Another difficulty of pursuing a dream is achieving a proper balance between realism and faith. Nothing is impossible with God, but He has given some clear guidelines in Scripture to help us determine the direction we should take.

Paul wrote to the Romans: "As your spiritual teacher I give this piece of advice to each of you. Don't cherish exaggerated ideas of yourself or your importance, but try to have a sane estimate of your capabilities by the light of the faith that God has given to you all" (Romans 12:3, PH).

As a little boy, I used to watch the buses loaded

with high school football players roll past our house on their way to a game. I dreamed of the day when I would be sitting in one of those buses and the kids along the street would be cheering for me.

But as a high school freshman, I choked back tears of embarrassment, frustration, and hurt when the football coach refused to even let me try out for the team. He said I was too small. "I couldn't live with my conscience because of what would happen to you out there," he said.

After several unsuccessful tries at basketball and track, my dream of athletic fame was shattered. I had never made a single team for which I tried out. The final showdown came during my junior year. I had a choice between one more attempt at the basketball team, or trying out for the junior play.

I took a good look at myself and decided that my gifts did not include athletics. My small body and my big-city high school were at odds with each other when it came to sports. But I had done well in some school plays and really enjoyed dramatics. It was either the locker room or the footlights, and I chose the stage.

God could have given me the determination to practice, try out, and maybe even make the basketball team. I really believe that. But when He made me, He didn't give me height or speed. He gave me other talents. It just took me a long time to admit it.

What has God given you? Have you used the faith He provides to make a sane estimate of your capabilities? (Romans 12:3) Or are you still clinging to a dream of being something else? By *faith* you can recognize God's hand of creation in your life, and agree that He knew what He was doing.

What are you good at? What do you enjoy? Where have you achieved a sense of satisfaction and accomplishment? That's probably the area in which you should begin to dream big and seek God's support to pursue excellence.

Motives Matter

"Never act from motives of rivalry or personal vanity, but in humility think more of each other than you do of yourselves. None of you should think only of his own affairs, but should learn to see things from other people's point of view" (Philippians 2:3-4, PH).

Behind every dream is a motive. Why do I want this? For what reasons am I pursuing this goal? Is it just for me? Do I want revenge? Do I want to show other people I can do it?

Hollywood columnist Rona Barrett, during her high school days once said: "Someday, so help me, I'll be so famous none of you will ever be able to touch me again" (Ralph Keyes, *Is There Life After High School?*, Warner Books, p. 109).

Fame might be motive enough for many people, but as Christians we have another consideration—pursuing God's plan for our lives, in His way. That eliminates a lot of motives like rivalry and personal vanity. Examining our motives is one way of having that "sane estimate" of ourselves according to the *faith* which God has given us.

Some dreams need to die. I don't want to discourage anyone who likes to dream big. But I really believe some dreams should die.

Many of our dreams may not be worth the effort it would take to turn them into reality. Not every dream is worthy of occupying the place of greatest importance in our lives.

Before taking his own life, Ralph Barton, a top cartoonist, left this note pinned to his pillow: "I have had few difficulties, many friends, great success; I have gone from wife to wife, and from house to house, visited great countries of the world, but I am fed up with inventing devices to fill up 24 hours of the day."

My childhood friend Doug (not his real name) had a similar attitude. His family had more money than any other family I knew. They lived in a huge home beside a lake, and it was always more fun to play there than at my house. In high school, we still considered ourselves good friends.

The summer after our freshman year in college, Doug was killed in an automobile accident. Early one morning he crashed his new Corvette at high-speed into a railroad track bed on a dead-end street.

I was working away from home that summer and never did find out exactly what happened. Some people I talked to later said Doug may have been drinking and didn't know where he was. Others said he knew exactly where he was and what he was doing. All I know for sure is that all his life Doug had everything that most people only dream about, but it wasn't enough.

If our dreams are centered on selfish pleasures and material things, they need to die and be replaced by ambitions that are real and lasting. Consider Paul's words to the Colossians: "Since, then, you have been raised with Christ, set your hearts on things above, where Christ is seated at the right hand of God. Set your minds on things above, not on earthly things" (Colossians 3:1-2).

Paul's advice isn't a call to check out of Planet Earth, but a challenge to see that our strongest desires are centered in Christ and His plan for our lives. We are to be involved in life here and now, but not all wrapped up in its everyday pleasures.

Guidelines for Dreamers

David wrote: "Do not fret because of evil men or be envious of those who do wrong; for like the grass they will soon wither, like green plants they will soon die away. Trust in the Lord and do good; dwell in the land and enjoy safe pasture. Delight yourself in the Lord and He will give you the desires of your heart" (Psalm 37:1-4).

Those are great guidelines for dreamers:

• *Don't envy those who ignore God and seem to have everything they want.* Their prosperity is temporary; yours is eternal.

• *Believe what God tells you, and put it to work in your life.* Start living right where you are, and enjoy the security that only the Lord can provide.

• *Discover for yourself what it means to really love God.* Nurture your relationship with Him, and He will become the motivation behind your desires and dreams.

The following excerpt of a mother's letter to her son, a college freshman, was printed in the *New York Times* (March 31, 1979): "What bothers me is that you don't seem to have any dreams anymore. There is nothing you want to do enough to put your heart and hand to it fully. Nothing that will get you out of bed before noon. Nothing that inspires you to want to be the best, or the first, or the only."

Do you have a dream? **Is** God the source and strength of that dream? If so, you can keep moving ahead confidently, in spite of all the temporary setbacks and obstacles you may encounter along the way.

When the Bottom Falls Out
4

Genesis 37:12-36

As I write this chapter, one of the books on the bestseller list is *When Bad Things Happen to Good People.* It deals with an age-old question: "Why does tragedy strike the lives of people who neither invite nor deserve it?"

Not long ago, four members of a Washington family were killed in a crash of their private plane. A neighbor expressed her anguish to a reporter by saying, "With all the creeps in the world, why did it have to be them?"

The Book of Job, one of the oldest in the Bible, deals with this same issue of the suffering of the righteous. Throughout Scripture we see people who loved God but faced sorrow in their personal lives.

Some excellent books have been written on the "why" of personal tragedy. But this chapter concentrates on the "how" of coping when "the bottom falls out." I'm sure Joseph must have done a lot of wondering about the "why" of his being sold into slavery. But if he hadn't chosen a good attitude and right actions in spite of that tragedy, we'd be studying someone else's life.

From Riches to Rags

As you read the account of Joseph's setbacks (Genesis 37:12-28), try to put yourself in his place. You're 17 years old, intelligent and good-looking, with big dreams for the future. Your brothers don't like you, but they know your father would never forgive them if they dared harm you. You feel safe around them.

Then one day, far from home and your father, things get out of hand. Your brothers' hatred has built up for so long that it explodes into a plot to kill you. For the first time in your life, you begin to believe they might go ahead and carry out their threats. You're afraid, and in spite of your cries for help and pleas for mercy, they seem determined to kill you.

Instead, your oldest brother Judah has a change of heart. He persuades the others to sell you to a traveling group of merchants for about eight ounces of silver. In the course of one day you have gone from being the privileged son of a wealthy father, through a brush with death, to being a common slave possessed by people you have never seen before.

If you saw the TV series "Roots," you might remember the reaction of Kunta Kinte, the young African who was captured and imprisoned by white slave traders. One day he was thrilled with freedom and the potential life held. The next day, he was trapped in a bamboo cage awaiting a voyage into the unknown. I wonder if Joseph didn't experience a similar conflict of emotions.

How can anyone cope with tragedy like that? I believe the first step is to have a realistic attitude toward life itself. We have to be prepared for the fact that things are going to go wrong, sometimes in a big way. Difficulties and obstacles are a fact of life, and they often hit us without warning.

Recently my family and I were driving in Montana when I saw a sign that said BUMP. No big deal. BUMP signs are common along the highway. There was no danger sign, no speed advisory, no word of warning; just the single word BUMP.

Two seconds later everyone in the car was hurled forward as I jammed on the brakes, trying in vain to slow down before hitting a four-inch rise in the level of the highway. I'm still surprised that the whole front end of the car didn't wind up in pieces along the roadside of Montana.

I wish that someone had explained the situation a little more thoroughly. Maybe the sign could have said, "Slow, 20 MPH." Or "four-inch concrete slab ahead. Slow down or destroy your car." Anything more than BUMP would have been appreciated.

Good News, Bad News

In life, we want all of our BUMP signs to have detailed explanations. Somehow, we have a craving for the truth about any situation, even if it hurts to face it. How many times have you encountered this line in a movie or book: "Just give it to me straight, Doctor." Or, "Don't try to pretend. If Tom means more to you than I do, just tell me."

Our desire for the brutal truth probably helped give rise to the "good news/bad news" jokes. You know the kind I'm talking about—like Sam, the Christian baseball pitcher. He wanted more than anything to know that some day he would get to play baseball in heaven.

An angel appeared to him one day and said, "Sam, I have some good news and bad news for you. The good news is that there is indeed baseball in heaven, and you will get to pitch."

"Great!" exclaimed Sam. "But what's the bad news?"

"You start on Thursday."

So let me give you the bad news first. If the bottom hasn't already fallen out of your life, it will. And if you've already experienced some major difficulties, don't get too relaxed. More will come. We live in a world that's messed up by sin and separation from God. Christians are subject to frustrations and disappointments just like everyone else.

The good news is that God can and does use even our worst experiences for His glory—if we let Him. Peter wrote some words of encouragement to Christians who had been forced to leave their homes. To those first-century refugees, he said:

"Dear friends, do not be surprised at the painful trial you are suffering, as though something strange were happening to you. But rejoice that you participate in the sufferings of Christ, so that you may be overjoyed when His glory is revealed" (1 Peter 4:12-13).

Perhaps the most supernatural thing about troubles in a Christian's life is that they don't have to lead to bitterness and despair. In fact, Peter says they should lead to rejoicing. But even though we can see the finish line, sometimes it still hurts to stay in the race.

Sorrow for a Christian is no less painful than it is for anyone else. When both of my parents suffered through cancer and died four years apart, I cried real tears and my stomach got tied up in real knots. There is no rule that says a Christian has to keep a stiff upper lip when life is at its toughest. God never expects us to pretend that bad things don't affect us.

Jesus wept at the tomb of His friend Lazarus. And the people who stood with Him said, "See how He loved him" (John 11:36). I don't think we can appreciate true rejoicing apart from the experience of deep sorrow.

I hope your parents live to enjoy their grandchildren and great-grandchildren, but they may not. I hope your family is healthy, that your brothers and sisters stay out of trouble, and that your parents' marriage is happy and strong. But you can't count on all those things happening because life is full of unexpected tragedies.

So what is the advantage of being a Christian during times of trouble? The difference is that Christians always have the hope of a better tomorrow. They may hurt. But God gives them the ability to pass through the sorrow into rejoicing. Everyone is going to have the tears and the disappointments, but where will they lead?

Through Sorrow

A number of years ago, we received news that our friends' 15-year-old daughter had been killed in an automobile accident. A group of young people were out driving after a football game, and the night ended in tragedy. The parents were shattered, overwhelmed by grief.

Years later we visited those parents who had moved to another state. They still kept one room in their home as "her room," furnished exactly as it had been before their daughter was killed. Her picture was on the dresser, her stuffed animals were on the bed, and I wouldn't have been surprised to find her clothes in the closet.

But the story doesn't end here. Through the influence of some friends, those parents became involved in Bible study and a caring fellowship of Christian people. They were able to talk about their tragedy, ask questions, and express their deep sense of loss.

They slowly experienced an inner healing far beyond anything they had ever dreamed possible. They were able to face the fact that their daughter is with Christ in heaven. For the first time in years, they no longer felt the need to keep a room in their home for the daughter they had lost.

God's promise is that we can keep moving through the sorrow into rejoicing. Instead of heaving a philosophical sigh that "everything will work out all right in the end," we can be confident that God is with us, working for our good and His glory through every situation.

"And we know that in all things God works for the good of those who love Him, who have been called according to His purpose" (Romans 8:28). Not we *think*, or we *hope*, but we *know*.

Throughout the Bible, we are assured that God loves us, knows everything that is happening in our lives, and has our best interests at heart. But sometimes it's hard for us to believe that. When things go wrong, we may know in our heads that God is still in control, but in our hearts it feels like He has disappeared. We need to be realistic about life, but we also need to be realistic about God.

In order to weather the storms of life, we must start to understand what God is really like. Without an accurate knowledge of who God is and how He works, we are always reevaluating our opinion of Him according to our current mood.

If we make the team, ace an exam, or win a scholarship, it's easier to feel that God loves us than when we fail in similar situations. When we're in love, God is wonderful. When we've just been dumped, we blame Him for not caring about us.

These minor problems often cause major doubts. What happens when we face major problems?

The bottom line is this: *What do I know about God that I will continue to believe no matter what happens? How can I be sure of God's love, even in the most difficult circumstances?* The answer to both questions brings me back to the Bible. It's not a book of magical answers, but it contains a bedrock source of truth about God.

Love That Lasts

Paul knew what he believed about God and His love: "For I am convinced that neither death nor life, neither angels nor demons, neither the present nor the future, nor any powers, neither height nor depth, nor anything else in all creation, will be able to separate us from the love of God that is in Christ Jesus our Lord" (Romans 8:38-39).

Neither death nor life. Just after Joni Eareckson Tada was paralyzed from the neck down in a diving accident, she wanted to kill herself, but couldn't. Still in her teens, she was totally helpless. In that state she preferred dying to living. But that was before she discovered the presence and power of Christ in her life. He helped her overcome her depression and gave her the will to live.

God's promise to us is that His love is greater than the obstacles of life and the certainty of death. Nothing can separate us from His love.

Neither angels nor demons. The Bible teaches that there is a great spiritual war being waged between the forces of good and evil. Whether we like it or not, we are a part of that warfare, involved in combat every day of our lives.

Often we lose key battles in that struggle. We see our best friends and family members wounded and hurting. The casualty lists grow longer. But God's promise is that even though battles may be lost, the war is already won. No enemy can separate us from the love of Christ.

Neither the present nor the future. Tragedy today often produces fear of tomorrow. "If this could happen today, then what could tomorrow bring?" "If that happened to a friend, it could happen to me."

God's promise is that today and tomorrow are in His hands. There is nothing which we are now facing or will ever have to face that can remove us from His love in Christ.

Nor any powers, neither height nor depth, nor anything else in all creation. Just in case he might have missed something, Paul covers all the bases in his last sweeping sentence. There is *nothing* that can pry me out of God's love in Christ Jesus.

Difficulty is the laboratory in which the truth of God's Word is put to the test. When tragedy hits, that's when we must learn for ourselves what we really believe about God. Will our faith fail or be strengthened by God?

Before and After

Remember what Jesus told His disciples before His crucifixion? "This very night you will all fall away on account of Me" (Matthew 26:31). And they did. Peter said that even though he might have to die with Jesus, he would never disown Him. But he did. When the soldiers came for Jesus, the disciples all ran away.

But do you also remember their courage after Christ had returned to heaven and sent the Holy Spirit to give them power? After being beaten with whips and ordered not to mention the name of Jesus again, "the apostles left the Sanhedrin, rejoicing because they had been counted worthy of suffering disgrace for the Name. Day after day, in the temple courts and from house to house, they never stopped teaching and proclaiming the Good News that Jesus is the Christ" (Acts 5:41-42).

The same men under the same pressure had a very different reaction. They were no longer afraid, but enjoyed a holy boldness in their approach to life.

The Holy Spirit who empowered them to press on in spite of difficulties also indwells and encourages us today. "For God did not give us a spirit of timidity, but a spirit of power, of love, and of self-discipline" (2 Timothy 1:7).

"But when He, the Spirit of Truth, comes, He will guide you into all truth. He will not speak on His own; He will speak only what He hears, and He will tell you what is yet to come. He will bring glory to Me by taking from what is Mine and making it known to you" (John 16:13-14).

The Spirit is the One who keeps reminding us of the unchanging love of Christ, no matter what the circumstances. The Holy Spirit encourages us to keep on trusting and following God, even when we want to quit.

Have you ever heard someone say, "Well, if that's the way God works, then count me out. If He lets things like that happen to good, innocent people, I don't want to have anything to do with Him." Most of us have felt that way at times.

But the essence of faith is that it continues to trust God even when things don't go the way we would like. "Now faith is being sure of what we hope for and certain of what we do not see" (Hebrews 11:1). Faith is the conviction, based on Scripture and encouraged by the Holy Spirit, that God is working for our good—even in the times and places where it seems least apparent.

Joseph was sold into slavery and hauled off to a foreign country to face an uncertain future. The years ahead of him looked grim. But the Lord knew what He was doing.

Joseph was a young man with deep faith in God. The bedrock of his life was the eternal, unchanging God of Israel. Even though circumstances had taken a drastic turn for the worse, Joseph was going to stick it out. God was the support of Joseph's life, and that foundation was as solid as it had ever been.

In this chapter we have seen Joseph dragged under the swift current of life and swept away. But in our next glimpse of him, he will have surfaced downstream, bruised but in one piece, still trusting in the God who is with him.

"Success" or Courage?

The people who stand out as heroes are not the ones who never have problems. Real heroes are people who demonstrate courage in facing obstacles.

A few years ago, a young Canadian named Terry Fox discovered that he had cancer. He was 18 when the surgeons amputated his right leg. For most young athletes, this would have been a total defeat. But not for Terry.

He determined to devote his life to a fight against cancer. He planned a "Marathon of Hope"—a 5,200 mile run across Canada to raise money for cancer research. On April 12, 1980 Terry dipped his artificial leg in the Atlantic Ocean and began his westward run.

In the next four and a half months, he ran more than 3,000 miles, to Thunder Bay, Ontario where he was forced to quit because his cancer had begun to spread. But his brave determination inspired his countrymen, and they responded to his courage. After Terry Fox's Marathon of Hope, Canadians contributed more than $24 million toward cancer research. When Terry died on June 21, 1981 the nation mourned.

Courage! That's what makes the world notice. We tend to think that our "success" will impress others and attract them to believe in Christ. But in reality, it is our faith and commitment to God when things are wrong, not right, that points others to the Saviour. While we might wish we could avoid the hard places in life, God wants to use them for our growth, our good, and His glory.

Even when "the bottom falls out," we still have a choice. We can choose to stick with God.

The Key to Opportunity
5

Genesis 39:1-6

One of my all-time favorite radio commercials begins with a ringing telephone which is answered by a plumber:

Plumber: Ace Plumbing Shop.
Woman: [*Very distraught*] Yes, I need some help. My kitchen sink is stopped up.
Plumber: Well, bring it in and we'll take a look at it.
Woman: You don't understand; it's my kitchen sink. It's attached to the wall. I can't bring it in.
Plumber: [*Aside to men in shop*] Hey, guys. This lady's sink is stopped up and she can't bring it in. [*Laughter in background*]
Woman: Can't you come out and fix it?
Plumber: I'm sorry, lady. We're pretty busy. If you can't get it in here, we can't help you.

Woman: Please, I'm having company for supper tonight. My husband's boss is coming.
Plumber: Well, don't take him into the kitchen. [*Click*]
Announcer: Seems like you just can't find good service anywhere these days. Except at _____ Motors. We don't just sell cars. We sell service.

Get It Yourself!

It seems we live in an age when "service" is rapidly becoming extinct. Our gasoline stations, discount stores, drugstores, and supermarkets are increasingly more self-service. If you want something, you have to get it yourself.

In America today, we are losing the art of serving. For some reason we have come to look down on those in service occupations. We treat those who serve us in restaurants with disrespect, give low status to maids, and would never think of listing "servant" as an occupational ambition.

Yet as Christians, you and I have been called to serve others. It is a command, not an option (Galatians 5:13-14). And in obeying that command we discover that service is a response that fits any situation.

The key to opportunity is choosing to serve. Of course, if you've read the Scripture for this chapter (Genesis 39:1-6), you've already found out that Joseph's new situation didn't look much like an opportunity. In fact, it looked more like a disaster.

After being sold by his brothers to a caravan of traders, Joseph was taken to Egypt and sold again. He was no longer treated as a person, but as property. He wasn't an intern, apprentice, or junior executive, but a slave. His new owner was a military officer named Potiphar, the captain of the king's guard.

A few weeks earlier, Joseph had expected a future as bright as his father's bank account. Now he was in a situation he never imagined could happen. He surely wouldn't have chosen such conditions for himself. If you were Joseph, what would you have done? He had a number of options.

Wrong Moves

Option 1: Escape. Right from the start, Joseph could have looked for a way out. He could have acted like a prisoner of war, giving only his name, rank, slave number, and date of birth. All the while, he could have been plotting his escape from Egypt and his way back home.

Option 2: Make trouble. He might have decided that the quickest way out of this bad situation would be to get himself thrown out. "I'll make them wish they'd never bought me as a servant. I'll sabotage this place," he might have reasoned. Then he could have proceeded to break the ashtrays, burn the bread, botch the gardening, and make a general mess of everything he was given to do.

Option 3: Complain. Joseph could have decided (perhaps unconsciously) that since he was stuck here, he might as well make everyone else around him miserable. He could have told his hard luck story to anyone who would listen, griped about the working conditions, and made himself the kind of person everyone tries to avoid.

Option 4: Do as little as possible. "Watch the clock. Mess around a lot. Only work when the boss is looking. Stretch each task to consume as much time as possible. Never do more than you are told to do. Insist on all your rights and benefits. Never volunteer." Joseph could have decided that since he didn't deserve to be there, then no one else should benefit from his misfortune.

Option 5: Manipulate and get what you can. "Go ahead and work hard, but just make sure you benefit more than anyone else. If there's nothing in it for you, don't do it."

These five options are the most common reactions to unpleasant situations. There are two problems with all of them: (1) they are unscriptural, and (2) they don't work. None of these options is an effective, biblical way of dealing with a difficult situation.

Escape. Often our first reaction to trouble is to want out. When we get a teacher we don't like, off we go to the counselor's office saying, "I can't stay in that class!" When our jobs get tough, we want to quit. Thousands of young people run away from home every year, shouting by their very actions, "I want out!"

The problem with escape is that it is never a good answer. More often than not, the circumstances aren't the problem. *We* are the problem. The cartoon character Pogo expressed it well when he said, "We have met the enemy and he is us."

Some of my life's most valuable lessons were

learned when my dad made me face some tough situations and see them through to the end, even when I wanted out. For instance, all through my sophomore year in high school, the only thing I wanted to get out of mechanical drawing class was me. But Dad made me stick it out and finish the course. And when I quit my summer job one night because I wanted to go swimming with some friends, Dad made me go to my boss, apologize, and ask to be rehired.

It was years later before I began to appreciate my father's wisdom, and how painful it was for him to watch me learn to press on even when it hurt.

Making trouble. Escape is not a healthy option and neither is causing trouble. The person who responds to difficulties by making trouble is described this way in Proverbs: "If a man digs a pit, he will fall into it; if a man rolls a stone, it will roll back on him" (Proverbs 26:27).

I remember a guy in my junior high school who was a constant troublemaker. He hated woodworking class, but it was required. So one day the guy glued all his tools into his toolbox. It got him out of woodworking class *and* out of school. The school made him pay for the tools, then expelled him. If making trouble gets us out of the frying pan, it usually gets us into the fire.

Complaining. One summer I worked with a classmate who was promptly nicknamed "Whiny" by everyone on the job. (Not "whinny" as in horse noises, but "whiny" as in "to complain in an annoying fashion.") He griped about everything to everyone, and when no one was listening, he complained to himself.

I don't think he enjoyed being a whiner, but he had formed the habit and was having a **hard** time breaking it.

Shirking and manipulation. Shirking and manipulation both fall into the category of self-centered approaches to difficult situations. Both are calculated strictly on the basis of, "What's in it for me?"

A Better Option

Weren't you surprised at how Joseph acted when he was sold to Potiphar? As a teenager, he showed more maturity in his attitudes and actions than a lot of adults. I don't know everything that went through Joseph's mind, but from his behavior it's obvious that he had decided to *serve.* What an option! What a choice!

Think for a minute about Joseph's choice. This 17-year-old had been the pampered son of a wealthy father. He could have had anything he wanted. But suddenly he's a slave, with no privileges and almost no free choice. Yet with the choice he *does* have, Joseph chooses to serve a stranger in a strange country—not because of his duty to Egypt, but because of his devotion to God.

As Joseph served God, the Lord gave him success in everything he did. And when Potiphar saw the results of Joseph's work, he put him in charge of his entire household. No option but service could have had such positive results.

W. Clement Stone, an expert on motivation, has said that "problems are merely opportunities in disguise." Evidently Joseph knew that truth centuries ago. But what really led to his rise from

The Key to Opportunity / 55

servant to superintendent in Potiphar's household? I believe the Bible gives us two reasons:

(1) "The Lord was with Joseph and he prospered" (Genesis 39:2). Here he was—favored by his father, hated by his brothers, sold into slavery, trapped in a foreign country, immersed in a strange culture, but *the Lord was with him.*

No matter what you're facing today, whether your life is peaceful or chaotic, grab hold of this truth: *There is no place where you can go or be sent where God isn't there already.* You will never find yourself in a situation where you are outside of God's presence.

The psalmist celebrated this great truth as he wrote:

Where can I go from Your Spirit?
  Where can I flee from Your presence?
If I go up to the heavens, You are there;
  if I make my bed in the depths, You are there.
If I rise on the wings of the dawn,
  if I settle on the far side of the sea,
even there Your hand will guide me,
  Your right hand will hold me fast
                    (Psalm 139:7-10).

If you have to move to a new city, change schools, go to live with one parent or the other, face the rejection of a friend, deal with the death of someone close to you, or whatever the circumstances, God is faithful and He is with you.

The promise of the Lord to all who know and trust Him is, "Never will I leave you; never will I forsake you" (Hebrews 13:5). Lots of people make that promise to each other and want with all their hearts to keep it, but fail to do so. The Lord is the only One who can make that promise and be fully trusted to never break it.

(2) Joseph made the choice to serve. As he served in Potiphar's household and took on more of his master's work, Joseph was not "doing what comes naturally." Serving is not a natural human response. Joseph's actions indicate a conscious decision to go "against the tide." His attitude determined his actions and changed the whole situation.

Why Serve?

(1) As Christians, we have been selected to serve. When Jesus' disciples began arguing about which of them was the greatest, He said to them:

"The kings of the Gentiles lord it over them; and those who exercise authority over them call themselves Benefactors. But you are not to be like that. Instead, the greatest among you should be like the youngest, and the one who rules like the one who serves. For who is greater, the one who is at the table or the one who serves? Is it not the one at the table? But I am among you as One who serves" (Luke 22:25-27).

Christ Himself has set the example and issued the command. His followers are to reflect His humility by their service to others.

(2) We have been set free to serve. Being a Christian is a liberating experience. Too often we see our faith as nothing more than a set of rules and regulations which take all the joy out of life. Nothing could be further from God's plan for our lives. But true freedom leads to service:

"You, my brothers, were called to be free," wrote

Paul. "But do not use your freedom to indulge the sinful nature; rather, serve one another in love" (Galatians 5:13).

A lot of your non-Christian friends think they're free, but they're not. It may look as if they have the freedom to go anywhere and do anything they please. But deep inside, they are slaves to their own sinful natures and are engaged in a never-ending search which can only end in frustration.

Without Christ, the bottom line of life is expressed in the hollow words of Mick Jagger and the Rolling Stones as they echo down two decades of indulgence, shouting: "I can't get no satisfaction."

There is no greater satisfaction than serving others with what God has given you—your time, talent, money, and happiness. It's not an easy lesson to learn, but it's worth learning.

People in Egypt who saw Joseph thought he was a slave, but in reality he was free. He had freedom to serve God and the people around him. In Christ, we have that same freedom to serve one another in love.

(3) We have been made secure to serve. It takes a secure person to serve others, and again, Jesus Himself has set the example.

"It was just before the Passover Feast. Jesus knew that the time had come for Him to leave this world and go to the Father. Having loved His own who were in the world, He now showed them the full extent of His love. The evening meal was being served, and the devil had already prompted Judas Iscariot, son of Simon, to betray Jesus. Jesus knew that the Father had put all things under His power, and that He had come from God and was returning to God" (John 13:1-3).

Pause a minute and think about the situation. Jesus knows this is His last night on earth. He is the leader, the teacher, the guest of honor.

He also knows that the Father has put all things under His power, that He has come from God, and is returning to God. What security! With all that power and importance, wouldn't you expect Jesus to sit back and relax while the disciples wait on Him?

"So He got up from the meal, took off His outer clothing, and wrapped a towel around His waist. After that, He poured water into a basin and began to wash His disciples' feet, drying them with the towel that was wrapped around Him" (John 13:4-5).

Washing the feet of the guests was the job of the lowliest servant in the household. No servant was present that night, and obviously none of the disciples had volunteered for the job, so Jesus washed their feet. He did it because He loved them, and to teach them how they should treat each other when He was gone.

You should have a great deal of security because of your faith in Christ. You know that someone loves and accepts you. You know that God is concerned about your everyday life. You know where you will spend eternity. This confidence should not produce personal conceit, but compassion for others. From our position of security in Christ, we can love and serve those around us.

Your Serve

Nathan C. Schaeffer has said it well: "At the close of life, the question will not be, How much have you got? but How much have you given? not How much have you won? but How much have you done? not How much have you saved? but How much have you sacrificed? It will be How much have you loved and served, not How much were you honored?"

Why not look now for some ways you can serve others? A natural place to begin is at home. Try anticipating the needs of others during mealtimes. Pass something their way instead of waiting for them to ask. Offer the last of a favorite dish or dessert to others before taking it all for yourself.

Conversation provides another great opportunity to serve. Most of us would rather talk than listen. Giving your undivided attention to someone is a rare compliment in today's noisy world.

How about social gatherings and school projects? Do you manipulate to get the best jobs and privileges, or are you willing to do the "dirty work" others try to avoid?

In your church youth group meetings, do you stick with your friends and hope newcomers find someone they know? Or are you willing to reach out and draw someone in, even if it means going outside your small group of special friends?

If you have a job, will your employer guess by your work that God is with you? He will if you serve.

In a difficult situation, Joseph recognized God's presence with him, and he turned disaster into opportunity by choosing to serve. We can make the same choice.

Life Without Walls
6

Genesis 39:6-23

If you could do anything you wanted, and you could be sure no one would ever know, what would you do? During junior high school, my best friend and I used to imagine a giant green fog putting everyone on earth to sleep, except my friend and me. People could awaken only when one of us touched them. Then they would do whatever we wanted and never remember it.

In our daydreams we destroyed schools, harassed teachers, bounced the bouncer at the movie theater, and indulged ourselves to the limit. Obviously, our primary concern was not the welfare of mankind.

A few years later I heard a speaker at a Christian conference say, "In the next few years, you will get the opportunity to do everything you have wanted to do. Whatever is in your secret heart of hearts," he said, "you'll have the chance to fulfill."

My first reaction was, "I can't wait!" But then I became concerned about my secret thoughts and the things I really wanted to do.

It has been more than 20 years since I heard that man speak, and time has confirmed the truth of what he said. Whatever we want, way down deep, the opportunity to get it is just down the road.

Barriers to Freedom

For years four main barriers have limited your freedom to choose.

(1) Parents: Your parents have set certain limits and made many choices for you. Their influence helps determine your friends, your activities, and your schedule.

(2) School: If it weren't for school, you would have another seven or eight hours each day to go where you want. But most jobs you will seek are going to require a level of education that will keep you in school for several more years.

(3) Friends: Your friends and peers influence your decisions. Peer pressure can be good or bad, depending on whose opinions and evaluations are important to you.

(4) The Law: Finally, the law limits your activities until you reach a certain age. The law governs driving, drinking, marriage, military service, and many other choices in our lives.

During your high school years, many of the barriers which have surrounded your life for so long begin to fall. You start to make more and more choices on your own. In a short time, most external restrictions on your power of choice will be gone, and you'll be free to do whatever you want. What will you do then?

The answer, with few exceptions, is that you will do whatever you *want* to. Someone has said, "Where desire meets opportunity, there occurs the act." Wise or foolish, good or bad, it's going to happen. The formula stands:

Desire + Opportunity = Action.

Since we can't control all of our opportunities, the key is in choosing the right desires. Life, in its most simple terms, is a matter of "want to."

How Could He Refuse?

Genesis 39 is one of the most significant "want to" chapters in the entire Bible. In it, we see Joseph's character put to the acid test.

How about a quick review of the situation? Joseph has risen from servant to superintendent in the house of Potiphar. Things are going so well that Potiphar lets Joseph make all the decisions about running the estate. Potiphar just shows up for meals.

According to verse 6 Joseph was well-built and handsome. I suppose that if most guys had a choice about having looks, brains, or money, most of us would go with the first. We can develop our minds and earn money, but if we aren't born with good looks, they're a little tough to acquire. The "cover" shouldn't be more important than the "book," but society has done a pretty good job of convincing us that good looks really count.

This part of Genesis begins to sound like "As the

Ancient World Turns." We read that Potiphar's wife went on a crusade to seduce Joseph. She wanted to have sex with him, and was determined to see that it happened. She offered the invitation not once or twice, but "day after day" (v. 10). Joseph avoided her as much as possible, but because of his job, he couldn't evade every encounter.

In his final confrontation with Mrs. Potiphar, Joseph gave two reasons for his refusal. First, his master trusted him. Nothing in the entire household was held back from Joseph except Potiphar's wife. Joseph refused to betray the trust that had been placed in him.

Second, Joseph firmly believed that to have sex with her would be to sin against God. No one else might ever find out, but God would know. Joseph didn't view God as some kind of cosmic chaperon, keeping him from having fun. Instead, he celebrated the fact that he could never get away from God, and wanted to avoid anything that would grieve his heavenly Father.

Joseph could have "gotten away with it." He could have rationalized his behavior and given lots of excuses, but his faith wouldn't let him. That is the secret of being true to God under any circumstances. When all the barriers were down, Joseph's "want to" carried him through.

Sex and the Single Student

Have you ever felt that God made a mistake in creating you so that your sexual energy is at a peak several years before you can get married?

64 / Free to Choose

Even though you are mature sexually, it may be 4 to 10 years before you will seriously consider marriage.

At the same time, you live in a world that says sexual expression is fine as long as you can avoid detection, infection, and conception. The popular speakers and books now proclaim that "nice girls do" and say that if two people really love each other, that's all that matters. But there is another side to that argument.

First, it's a fact that much of life involves saying no. It's just plain stupid to give ourselves everything we want, even though some people try to do just that.

The Old Testament describes what life is like for someone who never says no:

> Meaningless! Meaningless! ... Utterly meaningless!
> I denied myself nothing my eyes desired;
> I refused my heart no pleasure....
> Yet when I surveyed all that my hands had done and what I had toiled to achieve,
> everything was meaningless, a chasing after the wind; nothing was gained under the sun
>
> (Ecclesiastes 1:2; 2:10-11).

Dr. Armand Nicholi, Jr., a noted Christian psychiatrist, has said: "During the past 10 years I have noticed a marked change in the type of problems that bring young people to a psychiatrist. Previously, a great many came because of excessive inhibition of impulses. Today the opposite is true. The majority come because of an inability to control impulses."

Dr. Nicholi predicts that if current trends

continue, we will eventually have a higher rate of mental illness than ever before, with 90 percent of our hospital beds occupied by mentally ill patients. He says that "the nature of this illness will be characterized primarily by a lack of impulse control."

There's nothing wrong with saying no to your sexual desires before marriage. You won't go blind, lose your toenails, or permanently damage your personality. In fact, you'll still need to say no to yourself even after you're married.

For many young people, marriage looms ahead as some kind of sexual nirvana in which we are completely free to let our passions explode and run unbridled forevermore. If that's what you think, I have some more "good news and bad news."

The "good news" is that sex is a wonderful gift from God. He wants married couples to enjoy expressing their love and commitment to each other in a physical way.

The "bad news" is that sexual happiness and fulfillment aren't automatic. In fact, they don't have much chance of surviving apart from the emotional and spiritual oneness of a loving marriage relationship. And even in the best marriages, there are times when either partner may have to say no to sexual desire in order to really love and serve the other partner. Sex is infinitely more complex than "sleeping with" someone, "getting physical," or "doing it."

Marriage may be in the future for you. But what about now? How will you react as all those protective walls begin to fall?

One of the greatest pieces of advice in the Bible

is this: "Above all else, guard your heart, for it is the wellspring of life" (Proverbs 4:23).

Guard your "want to." Make sure that deep inside, what you want is what God wants. How?

In with the Good

One practical way is to keep a close watch on the input of your life. Some people say we *are* what we *eat*, physically. But what are you feeding on spiritually, day after day? What do you read, watch, listen to, and daydream about?

The psalmist said:
> How can a young man keep his way pure?
> > By living according to Your Word.
>
> I seek You with all my heart;
> > do not let me stray from Your commands.
>
> I have hidden Your Word in my heart
> > that I might not sin against You
> > > (Psalm 119:9-11).

One of the best ways to do that is through a systematic program of Scripture memory. The Topical Memory System published by The Navigators is one of the best available. I've always thought it strange that in our churches, we often push Scripture memory for little kids, then drop it for teens and adults. At this point in my life, I need God's Word hidden in my heart more than ever before.

It's time for a practical experiment. Before you read any further, go get a glass of water and put several drops of ink or food coloring in it. If you aren't standing at the sink right now, you're cheating.

There are several ways to get rid of that coloring in the water:

(1) You can empty the water into the sink. (Don't do it or you'll mess up the experiment.)

(2) You can find some chemical that would neutralize the color.

(3) You can place the glass under the faucet, turn on the water, and let it run. In just a little while the coloring will be gone, and the glass will be filled with fresh, clear water.

Imagine your mind as that glass. Every day you see, hear, and think things that pollute your mental "waters." It can't be helped. For the next few seconds, try to empty your mind of everything in it. (You're probably thinking that for some people this won't take long at all!)

But in most cases, the more you try to empty your mind, the more you remember the things you want to forget. It's better to *fill* your mind with fresh thoughts from God's Word which will gradually displace the polluted waters that produce some of our most destructive "want tos."

Scripture memory isn't a magic wand, but it is a good beginning toward the kind of desires that will produce the healthy, happy living that God wants for us.

What You're Looking For

Along the Oregon coast is a little place called Wee Willie's with a sign that reads, "Burgers, fries, shakes, home-baked pies."

Just past that sign is another one, erected by the Oregon highway department, that says, "Congestion." Both signs describe the same wide spot in the road, but they illustrate the dramatic difference that is made by someone's point of view.

If you're hungry and looking for a place to eat, Wee Willie's is a spot you'll look forward to. But if you're in a hurry, Wee Willie's is only a traffic jam where you need to dodge happy motorists full of burgers and fries.

In the summer, hundreds of people pass Wee Willie's every day. Some stop and others keep moving. It all depends on what they're looking for.

When Joseph was confronted with the opportunity to have sex with Potiphar's wife, he kept moving. It wasn't what he was looking for. He wasn't abnormal or full of psychological hangups. His temptation was real, but his "want to" was in tune with God's plan for his life. In this case he said no to a seemingly attractive opportunity because he was willing to say yes to God.

At this point in your life you are choosing the values that will carry you into a life "without walls." The barriers imposed by parents, peers, school, and laws have been valuable and important, but most of them are temporary. Now you must decide which direction you will go.

One ship drives east and another drives west
With the selfsame winds that blow.
'Tis the set of sails and not the gales
Which tells us the way to go
    (Ella Wheeler Wilcox, "Winds of Fate").

Where you go from here is where you really *want* to go.

Being Good, for Nothing?
7

Genesis 39:11-21

Let's be honest. When we follow the Lord and do what we know is right in a given situation, we *expect* things to go smoothly. But sometimes our right actions only seem to make things worse.

When Potiphar's wife tried to seduce Joseph, he did the right thing by saying no to her. He did what God wanted him to do. But look what happened. Mrs. Potiphar falsely accused Joseph of trying to rape her, and Mr. Potiphar had him thrown into prison. Some reward for following the Lord!

Take a close look at the progression of Joseph's life up to this point. Here is a young man trying to please the Lord in every area of his life, and we've seen him go from privileged son, to servant, and now to prisoner. The overall trend has been downhill.

Just when things seemed to be going well, *zap*!

The bottom fell out again. In his place, a lot of us might say, "Pardon me, but I'm getting off this sinking ship. If this is what happens when you serve the Lord, I'm ready to try something else."

We need to remember at this point that Joseph is in the *middle* of the story, not at the end. And that's precisely what we need to remember when our right actions produce changes for the worse. We haven't reached the end, either. There's more to come.

The Scenic Route

I was recently on a flight out of Denver late in the evening. As the plane left the runway and began climbing, I glanced down at the cars on the highway below. From my perspective, I could see just how far their headlights lit the roadway in front of them. The drivers could see only two or three car lengths ahead, yet they confidently sped along at, or above, the legal limit. It occurred to me that perhaps this is the way God sees us.

Here we are, driving down the road of life with only a vague idea of what's really happening around and ahead of us. Yet God, from His perspective, can see the beginning and the end. As we follow the route He has mapped out for our lives, we may have some delays and detours. But with patience, those detours will become God's "scenic route" to bring us to the place He wants us to be.

Choosing to trust God in the dark means accepting those God-given delays without concluding they are the end of the road. It means pressing ahead, in faith, even when we're not exactly sure what's happening or why. And sometimes, trusting God in the dark means learning to *wait* for His timing.

Microchip Christian?

In today's electronic society we seem convinced that we shouldn't have to wait for anything. Microwave ovens, home computers, and direct dialing are viewed as part of our inalienable right to immediate results.

The emphasis on immediate results has spilled over into many other areas as well. Psychologists have said that the current popularity of video games is directly connected to the fact that they give instant feedback. When you press a button, you know immediately how you're doing. You don't have to wait for a teacher to grade a test or for a friend to think about what you've said. You have an answer right now.

The prevailing mood of society is that whatever you want, you can have it *now*. People everywhere are saying:

• Don't wait until you have the money to buy something; get it *now* on credit.

• Don't save sex for marriage; enjoy it *now*!

• Don't waste time planning for the future; all you have is today. Do it *now*!

The trouble with this microchip mentality is that it just won't work in our relationships with Almighty God. Christian qualities—such as love, joy, peace, patience, and commitment—are slow to mature. Each characteristic must be carefully developed and continually nurtured. There is no such thing as push-button spirituality.

In Process

Time after time, the Bible encourages us to keep doing what is right long enough to get results.

"So do not throw away your confidence; it will be richly rewarded. You need to persevere so that when you have done the will of God, you will receive what He has promised" (Hebrews 10:35-36).

To persevere means "to persist or remain constant to a purpose or task in the face of obstacles" (*American Heritage Dictionary*). How far would you get in any challenging situation without perseverance? How many games would your team win? How many A's would you earn? How much money would you have in savings? It's a fact of life that when things don't happen easily or instantly, you just have to keep trying. The same principle applies to spiritual growth.

So how do we develop perseverence? The Apostle Paul describes the process this way: "We also rejoice in our sufferings, because we know that suffering produces perseverance; perseverance, character; and character, hope. And hope does not disappoint us, because God has poured out His love into our hearts by the Holy Spirit, whom He has given us" (Romans 5:3-5).

Take a closer look at the progression:
Suffering→Perseverance→Character→Hope

Personally, I find myself wanting hope without developing the first three steps. I want to spend 15 seconds in a spiritual microwave and instantly become a confident, optimistic person. But there's no spiritual shortcut that can produce hope.

In down-to-earth terms, perseverance is spiritual guts. When the coach tells you to "gut it out," he is telling you to keep going even when it hurts. Perseverance is the ability to overcome adversity, to go beyond what you thought you could endure.

Fall In

In December, 1968 I entered army basic training at Fort Ord, California. Every morning at 5:30 we lined up for a little "double time" run around the battalion area. It was dark, damp, and cold at that time of day.

None of us was thrilled with the exercise, but for two guys in our platoon it was a time of total agony. Both were very overweight, and the only regular exercise they were used to was bending over to see what was in the refrigerator. In the course of the one- or two-mile morning run, both of them would "fall out" and come dragging in well after the rest of us.

But as we continued our sessions, one of those guys began to make it a little farther each day. His suffering produced perseverance. By the end of basic training he could complete the entire run, and he graduated with well-earned pride in his new endurance.

The other guy continued to give up at precisely the same point each time, even though we did everything we could to help him. We even put the biggest guys in the platoon on both sides of him, and literally carried him around the track until the drill sergeants saw it and made us quit.

The overweight soldier could have become

stronger each day if he had been willing to push himself. But his mind refused to believe that he could run any farther than the day before. He was placed in a special training company, and as far as I know he never finished basic training.

"No discipline seems pleasant at the time, but painful. Later on, however, it produces a harvest of righteousness and peace for those who have been trained by it" (Hebrews 12:11).

Through suffering we can develop perseverance—if we don't try to short-circuit the process.

Character-istics

"Suffering produces perseverance; perseverance, character...." Our repeated perseverance produces *character*—what we are down deep inside. Character is revealed by what we do when no one is looking. As D.L. Moody has said so well: "Character is what you are in the dark." Character determines how we respond to "life without walls," when the temporary barriers restricting our choices are gone.

Perseverance produces character *one choice at a time*. We are the sum total of the hundreds of choices, good and bad, we make each day. The more often we choose correctly, even when we are not immediately rewarded for it, the stronger our characters become.

Character gives us the freedom of knowing that our behavior is not determined by our circumstances. In daily living, character means that:

- Honesty, not deception, characterizes our lives at all times.

- We have a single standard of behavior; not one for our parents and youth leaders, and another for our friends at school.
- Our "walk" matches our "talk."
- We can move confidently ahead in life without keeping our eyes on the rearview mirror to see if anyone is watching.

Finally, character produces hope. Christians believe that God has unlimited power to work in our world and our lives. Nothing is too hard for Him. But we also realize that He never *forces* His way on any of us. We are free to choose whether we will follow or turn away from Him.

Maybe you've wondered whether you might let God down at some point because you might lack the strength to choose the right way. I guess we never gain total confidence in our ability to always make the right choices.

But as suffering produces perseverance, and perseverance builds character, we can develop *hope* to face the days ahead.

"If God gave me strength to follow Him through this difficult time," we conclude, "then He can take me through anything." Our hope is not in ourselves, but because God's grace and mercy have brought us through in the past, we can trust Him for the future.

Suffering→Perseverance→Character→Hope

Maybe you've already been through this process, and have developed hope for the future. Great! Does that mean you'll never again face suffering? Of course not.

The cycle starts all over again. But once you have developed hope, you can use it the next time you face suffering. And once you discover that you are "in process," it frees you from the need to be rewarded immediately for every good choice and action. As you look back on your life, you'll be able to see God's wisdom in the way He has led you.

"Let us not become weary in doing good, for at the proper time we will reap a harvest if we do not give up" (Galatians 6:9).

What's in It for Him?

A great deal of teaching and writing today is centered on "What we get for serving Jesus."

From the "What's In It For Me" department, we hear things like:
- Believe in Jesus and make the team.
- Follow Jesus and become a cheerleader.
- Become a Christian and improve your grades.
- Give your life to Christ and break the record, get elected, have more money, more fun, more friends....

I believe we need to recapture the idea that following Christ is not for us; it is for *Him*.

Jesus told His disciples: "You did not choose Me, but I chose you to go and bear fruit—fruit that will last" (John 15:16).

Somehow it seems that we have reversed the roles and tried to make God the One who is supposed to keep bearing fruit for us. We try to make prayer our computer link to a great shopping center in the sky from which we can order the things we want. While there is much to be gained by following Christ, the motive of getting things *from* Him will never stand the test of hard times.

God has called us to be part of a great success story, but on His terms, not ours. We often decide what we want for ourselves, then advise God how to make it happen. If events don't go our way, we become disillusioned with God.

That could have happened to Joseph. What a disappointment to rise from rookie slave to estate manager, only to have his success destroyed by the sin of someone else. It was unjust, unfair, and beyond understanding. Life must have seemed to Joseph like a house of cards, fragile and ready to collapse at the slightest tremor.

But the story isn't over yet. "While Joseph was there in the prison, the Lord was with him" (Genesis 39:20-21).

Buried, Alive

This is the second time in this chapter of Genesis that we have found Joseph buried under the rubble of life which has tumbled down around him. First he was made a slave, then he was accused unjustly. Yet in both cases that single phrase, "the Lord was with him" was the ray of hope that shone through, even when things looked darkest.

Joseph is still "in process." He hasn't given up, hasn't abandoned ship, and hasn't tried to escape the working of God in his life. Instead, he is still trusting, even when he can't see anything good in his future.

Joseph is learning to wait. His suffering is developing perseverance, character, and hope that will not disappoint him in the days ahead.

How about your life? Have you accepted the

challenge of obeying the Lord, only to have things get worse? Have you suffered someone's false accusation and been punished for something you didn't do? Have you struggled back from a bitter disappointment only to have the rug pulled out from under you again?

Remember that God isn't playing games, seeing how confused He can make you. He loves you and is at work in your life to develop the qualities that will help you bear fruit for Him.

When right actions seem to produce wrong results, we still have a choice. We can trust God in the dark.

On Top of the Bottom
8

Genesis 39:21-40:8

A few years ago, I took my junior high students on a field trip to the county jail. (I often wondered if some of them hadn't been there before.) We got off the school bus, trooped down the long ramp where the sheriff's cars drive in, and went into the booking area.

Everyone was having a great time. There was a lot of horseplay and joking around. From the booking area, we walked through an interrogation room and into a long hallway. A deputy showed us the shower stall where all prisoners were required to strip and undergo a disinfecting shower to prevent lice in the jail. The hallway reeked with the overpowering smell of chemical disinfectant.

Suddenly, from behind us, came the loud metallic clang of the security door being closed. The talking and laughing stopped. The closing of that door was a sobering sound. We were locked in, and it made all of us wonder what it would be like to be really imprisoned instead of guided through on a field trip.

We moved past some holding cells—concrete boxes with bars on three sides, a cot in one corner, and a toilet hanging off the back wall. There was not even a hint of privacy. No one in our group talked, no one laughed, no one thought it was funny. No one said a word until we were outside the jail.

I don't know if you have ever visited any prisons, but they are not *happy* places. They are filled with people who have lost their freedom, mostly because they didn't make the right choices. Some prisoners, no doubt, are victims of a breakdown of justice and are being held unfairly. In either case, jail is a place people want to leave as quickly as possible.

Faithful Felon

I wonder how Joseph felt when his prison door closed behind him. We don't know much about the place where Pharaoh's prisoners were confined, but we do know it changed when Joseph arrived. It became a better place than ever before, because God was with him.

Can others say the same thing about you? When you face difficult situations do people around you notice God's presence in your life?

Even in prison we see Joseph *serving* his way into a position of trust and responsibility. "The Lord ... showed him kindness and granted him favor in the eyes of the prison warden" (Genesis

39:21). Here is a pattern we would all do well to imitate. When in doubt, serve! When we don't quite know how to approach people and circumstances, serve! Serving others is always an appropriate response.

"So the warden put Joseph in charge of all those held in the prison, and he was made responsible for all that was done there. The warden paid no attention to anything under Joseph's care, because the Lord was with Joseph and gave him success in whatever he did" (Genesis 39:22-23).

I would think one of the next worst alternatives to being *in* a prison is being *in charge of* one. What a nightmare! There you are trying to organize a place full of people who don't want to be there. Many of them have nothing to lose by trying to break out. The warden is paying no attention to what's going on. He's picking up his paycheck, you're doing all the work, and he's getting all the credit. If everything goes well, there's nothing in it for you. If a riot breaks out, they'll have your neck. What a job!

Yet Joseph made another crucial choice which kept him on track with God's plan for his life. Even in the midst of great personal difficulty, he chose an attitude that allowed him to help others.

When Joseph's story is read from a strictly human point of view, it doesn't seem that he is making much progress. In a very real sense, he has risen to the top of the bottom. He has become the chief servant of people in trouble, and he can see no opportunity for advancement. He must have listened to a lot of hard-luck stories during the years he was there, but I can't imagine that any of the others could top his own.

Crummy Little Jobs

In the army, we had a similar position—"crummy little jobs officer" (term modified for Christian publication). Every second lieutenant has had a small dose of that job. In my first unit, I was designated transportation safety officer, fire safety officer, unit historian, and custodian of the emergency medical kit. The titles sound impressive, but in reality I was in charge of the things no one else wanted to be responsible for. As young officers, we figured the top brass needed someone to blame when things went wrong.

Then two things happened to change my mind and teach me the importance of "the little things" in life.

One day an old warehouse caught fire and burned to the ground. An investigation revealed that the cause of the fire had been some oily rags improperly stored inside the warehouse. But the fire had spread rapidly because of an artillery round that exploded!

Oily rags are a "no-no" in the first place, but there was no excuse for storing an artillery shell in a warehouse. Some poor second lieutenant fire-safety officer for that building is probably still trying to explain that one.

Someone long before had probably stored all that junk improperly, but the young officer had accepted responsibility for the building. He should have visited the warehouse, taken inventory, and corrected the problems.

A second event that focused my attention on the importance of little things hit closer to home. During an inspection in our barracks, someone discovered that all the fire alarm hammers had been filed off, and the alarms were impossible to activate. If fire had broken out, there was no way to warn people in the barracks and summon the fire department.

Do you remember who our fire safety officer was? That's right. The inspection team sat *me* down in a room and asked me *why*?

I certainly hadn't filed down the alarm hammers, and I had no idea who had. But because it had become my responsibility, they were going to make sure I got the blame. I finally found out that the alarm hammers had been removed years before because they kept snagging on uniforms and turning in false alarms. We repaired the system and I learned three important lessons.

Big "Little Things"

My first lesson was that *little things are important*. Jesus said that, "Whoever can be trusted with very little can also be trusted with much" (Luke 16:10). But we can become so interested in getting a big break that we neglect the details of life.

How do you suppose Joseph's warden knew that the Lord was with Joseph? How did he decide that Joseph could be given added responsibility? It must have been obvious from everything about Joseph, including the details of his life.

How do you handle details? For instance:
- The arrangement of your closet?
- The cleanliness of your room?
- How about your table manners and the way you treat your family and friends?

- How faithful are you in fulfilling responsibilities at home, church, and school?
- How's your record of finishing the things you start?
- How's your job performance? Would your employer recommend you to someone else?
- What about your daily time alone with the Lord, reading His Word and praying?

When all of these "little things" are combined, they provide some important indicators of how well you'll handle bigger things when they come along.

Live Today

The second lesson I learned was to *build my life on the reality of today, not on the anticipation of tomorrow*. Anticipation is a wonderful thing that helps keep life interesting, but it can also rob us of today.

What are you looking forward to right now? Are you counting the days until something special happens? The beginning of your favorite sport? A holiday? Vacation? A date with that special person? Graduation?

Great! I hope your life is filled with anticipation. But what are you doing in the meantime? Let's face it, most of our lives are made up of ordinary days. What we accomplish and what we become is the result of how we use those ordinary days when nothing much seems to be happening.

What if Joseph had sat around in prison waiting for his big break? He could have hoped that Potiphar would discover the truth and have a change of heart. Maybe Pharaoh would drop by for a visit sometime and Joseph could tell the ruler how he had been framed.

Instead of wasting his time in anticipation, Joseph began taking each day as it came and responding to the opportunities in each one. It didn't matter that he was unable to achieve fame and fortune; he was content with his opportunities to serve.

I have a friend in Bolivia, who is translating the Bible into the language of the Guayaru Indians. He has been there for 10 years and has just completed translating the New Testament. What an accomplishment!

How did he do it? One day at a time. He began by learning their language and producing a written alphabet for them. Then he began with one verse, then a chapter, then a book from the New Testament. Each was a small opportunity on an ordinary day filled with ordinary things but the end product was no little achievement.

Hidden Opportunities

Finally, I learned that *many of our greatest opportunities come to us disguised as problems.* The things I'd rather avoid in life seem to teach me the most. Haven't you found the same to be true?

One day while Joseph was making his rounds in the prison, he noticed that two men looked more dejected than usual. (They must have been *really* depressed.) So he asked them why they were so sad (Genesis 40:6-7).

Can you imagine that? Here's a man whose life

has been one problem after another. In prison, he's heard more hard-luck stories than a bartender in the Bowery, and he still stops to ask two prisoners why they are feeling so sad. The incredible thing is that Joseph probably really wanted to know. His concern was real and the two men sensed it.

A high school student told me about his concern for witnessing to his friends at school. "I'm frustrated," he said, "because they don't seem interested in listening to me or the Gospel."

I know just how he feels. It's a common problem for all of us in sharing the Gospel with those we know. But I've come to the conclusion that the root of the problem is trying to divorce witnessing from really caring about other people. I often want to tell others *my* testimony without listening to their stories.

Joseph blended his caring and sharing in such a beautiful, natural way. It's an encouraging lesson for all of us. He saw people with needs and he reached out to meet them. By asking, "Why are you feeling so sad?" he initiated a conversation about the dreams that caused them such worry. Then in the process of helping them understand their dreams, he gave credit to God for the ability to interpret them. He pointed them toward the One who was not only the source of specific information, but the Creator and Lord of all.

What began as a problem—two sad prisoners—quickly became an opportunity for personal witness. Most of us tend to forget about God when things are going well. It is during the times when our lives show signs of cracking and falling apart that we are most responsive to the voice of God.

Keep Your Eyes Open

Many opportunities God gives you to witness for Him in your school will begin with your sensitivity toward someone in need and your willingness to reach out and help. It may be the student-body president or it may be the girl who sits alone at lunch every day. It may be the person with a thousand friends or the loner who has none. Your first clue may be that same look of sadness which Joseph saw on the faces of the two prisoners in his care.

Too often in life we try to manipulate circumstances, get the big breaks, and strengthen our own position. But sometimes helping others is really the best way to reach our goals.

We look at the ordinariness of our daily lives and our chances to serve and say, "There's no future in that." But that's exactly where our future is if we could only see and grab hold of the opportunities that are there.

Two passages of Scripture express this principle of growing through giving:

"One man gives freely, yet gains even more; another withholds unduly, but comes to poverty. A generous man will prosper; he who refreshes others will himself be refreshed" (Proverbs 11:24-25).

"Remember this: Whoever sows sparingly will also reap sparingly, and whoever sows generously will also reap generously. Each man should give what he has decided in his heart to give, not reluctantly or under compulsion, for God loves a cheerful giver. And God is able to make all grace abound to you, so that in all things at all times, having all that you need, you will abound in every good work" (2 Corinthians 9:6-8).

Remember Joseph, the victim of major wrongs and injustices. Of course he was disappointed that he was in prison. Of course he wanted out. But instead of wishing his life away, he continued his pattern of faithfulness in the little things of life. He took every opportunity that came his way to offer help and encouragement to those around him.

Even when he was only on top of the bottom, he made the choice to help others.

Let Down Again
9

Genesis 40:9-23

It has been said that the measure of a person is determined by what it takes to make him give up. What does it take to stop you—at home, at school, at work, at church, at play? At what point do you say, "I quit! I've had it. It doesn't make any difference what I do, so I just won't try any more."

Amazingly, the Bible doesn't record any time in Joseph's life when he reached that point of giving up. We don't know how close he may have come to it, but the important thing is that time after time, when circumstances refused to improve, Joseph chose to keep on trying.

We've already seen that Joseph had more reasons to give up on life than most of us will ever have. In this chapter he faces another one. Read Genesis 40:14-23, and meet the king's cupbearer—a nice guy with a short memory.

After Joseph interpreted the dreams of the

cupbearer and the baker, he asked the cupbearer to do him a simple favor. "When all goes well with you, remember me and show me kindness; mention me to Pharaoh and get me out of this prison. For I was forcibly carried off from the land of the Hebrews, and even here I have done nothing to deserve being put in a dungeon" (Genesis 40:14-15).

But when his fortunes improved and he was restored to Pharaoh's service, the cupbearer didn't remember Joseph. He forgot him.

Who Can You Trust?

At this point, if I had been Joseph, I might have come to one of the following conclusions:

Conclusion #1: *You can trust God, but you can't trust people.* Not long ago, I saw a little sign which said: "In God we trust. All others have to pay cash." In Joseph's place, it would have been easy to accept that kind of thinking.

Have you begun to notice a certain trend in Joseph's story? For the past decade, almost every significant person in his life has let him down. His own brothers, a member of the opposite sex, his employer, and now a friend have all disappointed him. How long could you put up with that before you became convinced that people were not to be trusted?

Conclusion #2: *You can't trust anyone, God included.* When misfortune strikes, we want to blame someone. If we feel that we haven't done anything to deserve it, then it must be God's fault. When it happens more than once, we may be tempted to shake our fists at God and say, "If this is how You treat people who serve You, then count me out!"

Conclusion #3: *If you want something to happen, make it happen yourself.* Have you ever given God a time limit? "If You don't do something about this by 3:30 tomorrow afternoon, God, then I'll handle it myself!" There is nothing wrong with initiative, but life is full of situations where the best thing we can do is wait on God. And while we wait on God, we should concentrate on becoming the kind of people He wants us to be.

Sometimes waiting involves trusting another person. If we become convinced that neither God nor other people can help us, then we're in for a long, hard life. It's a lonely existence to be the only one in the world you can trust.

The Bible gives no evidence to indicate that the cupbearer's forgetfulness made Joseph change his way of life. Sure, he must have been disappointed when days, weeks, months, and finally two years went by with no word from the palace. But Joseph never gave up. He knew that when God's time was right, things would begin to happen.

Why was Joseph able to wait and be ready for his opportunity when it came? I believe it was because he was free from the need to have an instant reward for following God. Most people operate under a "cost/benefits" theory of daily living. Under this approach, every choice they make is based on two questions: "What will it cost me?" and, "What can I get out of it?"

If the costs outweigh the *immediate* benefits, forget it!

Most of us use the "cost/benefits" theory in our approach to daily living. Think about:

Friendships. How many completely one-sided friendships do you have? Aren't most of them based on a mutual give-and-take? Friendship is costly, but we also gain a lot from it. We keep "paying" as long as the *costs* don't outweigh the *benefits.*

School. Suppose you decide to take an accelerated class under a difficult teacher. You know the cost is going to be high in terms of time and effort. But you also know that it is the best way to get a scholarship.

Sports. You cannot get yourself into top physical condition without undergoing pain. It hurts to exercise and practice. But that's the price you have to pay if you want to win.

The question is, how did Joseph endure when his costs seemed so much higher than his benefits? Why did he remain faithful to the Lord when his world kept falling apart?

Costs, Benefits

Joseph believed that no matter what he was going through, the benefits eventually would outweigh the costs. The key word here is *eventually*. It removes the tremendous burden of wanting a quick reward for every action. It enables us to maintain a positive attitude and spiritual stability today, because we know tomorrow is in God's hands.

If you are a student, think of the money you could be earning if you weren't going to school. In one sense, it is costing you a lot to be in school instead of working. But in terms of your future earning power, you are actually making money by completing your education. The benefits of graduating from high school or college outweigh the immediate costs involved.

The same principle holds true in our Christian lives. When we are obedient to God, we give Him the right to determine both the costs and the benefits of our lives. We believe His way will be the best way, even if we don't understand how. We choose to keep serving Him, no matter what.

"Whatever you do, work at it with all your heart, as working for the Lord, not for men, since you know that you will receive an inheritance from the Lord as a reward. It is the Lord Christ you are serving" (Colossians 3:23-24).

When we choose our attitudes and actions in the light of that truth, we are saying to the Lord: "You outline the job and set the salary. I'll be happy with whatever You decide. If it seems that my pay is less than I deserve, and even if it decreases, I'll still be confident that You know what You are doing. You will make it right for me eventually." Most of us would gladly let God set the "costs" in our lives, as long as we could choose the "benefits."

I once spoke at a church conference on Hebrews 11:6: "Without faith it is impossible to please God, because anyone who comes to Him must believe that He exists and that He rewards those who earnestly seek Him."

After the meeting, a woman approached me and said she couldn't agree with that passage of Scripture. "After what has happened in my life during the last few months," she said, "I can't see that God rewards those who earnestly seek Him. I think the Bible should say that 'God is with them,' but I can't believe the part about the reward." We discussed the passage for a while and came to this conclusion: Maybe God being with us *is* the reward.

Most of us tend to think of reward in terms of comfort, security, or material possessions, but God's presence with us can be reward enough. It was for Joseph. His willingness to let God determine his costs and benefits enabled him to handle setbacks and overcome some deep disappointments.

Tailspin

Disappointment is usually a reaction to specific events. When we fail a test, lose the game, or don't get invited to the party, naturally we're disappointed. It's one of those things we can't avoid in life, and it's nothing to be ashamed of. But if we don't bounce right back, disappointment can begin a long emotional spiral downward.

The next level downward is *discouragement*. We can lose confidence and spirit, and develop a negative view of life. Discouragement can make us hesitant to try new things for fear of failing. If we don't deal with our discouragement, it can lead us further down the emotional scale.

The next level is *depression*—a long-lasting attitude of dejection that affects our outlook on everything around us. It produces a kind of mental pressure that distorts the truth. Everything seems worse than it really is.

Depression is serious, but *despair* is critical. Despair is the loss of all hope—the point at which we give up, throw in the towel, and quit trying. It is one of the saddest conditions of life.

Signs of despair are all around us. The rate of teenage suicide is now higher than ever before. Faced with competitive peer pressure, difficult family situations, distorted sexual values, and a society that sometimes seems to be crumbling around them, a lot of young people are simply giving up. They look at their lives, their families, and their world and say, "It isn't worth it. I give up. I'm checking out."

Dr. Bennett Leventhal of the University of Chicago says: "Most of us in the mental health field believe that suicide is the leading cause of death among adolescents and that they probably have the highest suicide rate of any age-group. It is a frightening and very serious problem" (Ronald Kotulak, *Chicago Tribune*).

But let's back up a minute. How can we avoid despair, and the problems it can bring? The best place to deal with this emotional spiral is at the disappointment level. We must avoid letting our disappointments pile up and push us down into discouragement and depression. The key is to keep "short accounts" with God and with each other. When something happens that disappoints us, we need to work it through and settle it right away.

Sometimes this will mean talking with the other people involved. In other cases, it will be a matter of bringing our feelings to the Lord and settling the issue with Him. Peace comes when we accept His plans for our lives and tell Him we will keep following Him, no matter what.

All of us have limits of "what we will take" before giving up. Part of God's work in our lives is to extend those limits, for our good and His glory.

Ordinary People

Personally, I would like to be a smashing success on the first try of everything I do. I often think that would impress people around me and even cause them to see that God is present in my life. But that isn't how God works.

How impressed with God's power would you be if Joseph never had any problems? Imagine he graduated from high school as valedictorian of his class, and then earned his Master's Degree in four years with a double major in agriculture and economics. Following that, he earned his Ph.D. in international relations. After sending his college transcripts to several countries, he was hired by Pharaoh and made second in command of the entire country of Egypt.

Pretty impressive, huh? But we couldn't identify with that kind of person. He would have to be a genius, and we're just ordinary, garden-variety human beings. The world only takes notice when it sees someone who has every reason to give up, but keeps on trying. Some of the best-known figures in history have had to overcome staggering setbacks in life.

Take a look at Abraham Lincoln's record before he was elected President in 1860:

In 1831, he failed in business.

In 1832, he was defeated for the Illinois State Legislature.

In 1833, he again failed in business.

In 1834, he was elected to the legislature.

In 1836, he proposed to Mary Owens, and she turned him down.

In 1838, he was defeated for speaker.

In 1840, he was defeated for elector.

In 1843, he was defeated for Congress.

In 1846, he was elected to Congress.

In 1855, he was defeated for Senate.

In 1856, he was defeated for Vice-President.

In 1858, he was defeated for the Senate.

Before Helen Keller was two years old, an illness destroyed her sight and hearing. Yet she overcame her physical handicaps, learned to speak and write, and became internationally known as a champion for the rights of the handicapped.

As Christians, God has not promised us a problem-free existence. But He has promised to be with us in every situation to provide the strength we need. He has also promised that, down the road, our trust in Him will be rewarded.

When the Apostle Peter wrote a group of Christians who were suffering because of their faith, he said: "In this you greatly rejoice, though now for a little while you may have had to suffer grief in all kinds of trials. These have come so that your faith—of greater worth than gold, which perishes even though refined by fire—may be proved genuine and may result in praise, glory, and honor when Jesus Christ is revealed" (1 Peter 1:6-7).

We live in a strange time when people have grown accustomed to the idea that God will reward His followers with wealth and comfort in this life. Historically, Christians have expected joy and peace from their Lord, not material things. Perhaps we need to recapture that perspective.

No Substitute

Joseph knew that his benefits would eventually outweigh any "costs" of personal sacrifice. That truth helped him remain faithful to God. A second reason for his faithfulness was that he saw forsaking the Lord as an unacceptable alternative.

If you decided to toss your Christian faith aside, what would you replace it with?

Pleasure? It's out there and lots of folks are on that pathway of life. The door is open for whatever you want, and there's a lot of mystery and excitement in exploring the things you've never experienced.

Humanism? A lot of folks claim that God is the invention of weak people who couldn't make it on their own. They say that the answers to life are within yourself. So you can take a deep breath, pull yourself up by your bootstraps, and press on.

Another religion? You can probably find one that professes to "explain and answer" all the things that Christianity doesn't. You may even find a religion that allows you to do whatever you want without any restrictions.

Joseph could have made similar choices, but he didn't. He saw anything less than total commitment to the true God as an unacceptable option.

Joseph understood the futility of life outside of God's will. The Prophet Jeremiah expressed this futility when he wrote these words about the nation of Israel: "My people have committed two sins: they have forsaken Me, the Spring of Living Water, and have dug their own cisterns, broken cisterns that cannot hold water" (Jeremiah 2:13).

When Jeremiah wrote these words, water was a matter of life and death. How absurd it would be to abandon an artesian spring and carve a cistern out of rock, only to discover that it was full of cracks and couldn't hold water. It would be not only tragic, but deadly.

If you saw a new car that looked like a Rolls-Royce advertised for $800, you'd be suspicious. It might look good on the outside, but it would be nothing but a cheap imitation, and it would never hold up as well as the original.

There are a lot of options outside the Christian faith, but no good ones. There are many ways to respond to the hard places in life. But only one Way keeps us in tune with the plans and purposes of God.

Remember the incident in Jesus' life when His teaching caused a number of His followers to turn back and no longer follow Him? John records what happened next when Jesus spoke to His inner core of disciples:

" 'You do not want to leave too, do you?' Jesus asked the Twelve. Simon Peter answered Him, 'Lord, to whom shall we go? You have the words of eternal life' " (John 6:67-68).

What a beautiful response! "Us, leave? Where would we go? To whom would we turn? There are no other good alternatives. You are the only One who has the words of eternal life."

Coming Back

The American Heritage Dictionary defines *resilience* as (1) the ability to recover quickly, as from illness; buoyancy, and (2) the property of a material that enables it to resume an original shape after being bent or stretched.

You can see resilience all through Joseph's life. He's knocked down, but right back on his feet; betrayed, but still trusting the God who is with him; in captivity, but free to help and serve the people around him; disappointed, but never abandoning the course of faith and service he has chosen.

God is at work producing resilience in us too. Sure, the process is painful. No one likes being wadded up and thrown into the corner, stretched out of shape, or flattened under pressure. Sometimes we feel like the guy who was run over by a steam roller, and then placed in the hospital—in rooms 115-119.

But resiliency comes when we accept *God's* cost/benefit program for our lives, and when we recognize that there is no need to turn away from Him to seek a better alternative. Just when we think we can't take it anymore, God provides all the grace and strength we need.

"We do not want you to be uniformed, brothers, about the hardships we suffered in the province of Asia. We were under great pressure, far beyond our ability to endure, so that we despaired even of life. Indeed, in our hearts we felt the sentence of death. But this happened that we might not rely on ourselves but on God, who raises the dead" (2 Corinthians 1:8-9).

Disappointments will come. Yet even when it seems the bad times may never end, we still have a choice. Like Joseph, we can turn in faith to God, trusting that His way is best, and choose to keep on trying.

How to Handle Success
10

Genesis 41:1-57

In army basic training, nothing is lower than private E-1's. For the first few weeks, they are less than human, the scum of the earth, and can do nothing right. They are rarely addressed by name, and usually answer to a series of unflattering terms which exist only in a drill sergeant's vocabulary.

Besides that, its a *long* way up the ladder of promotion. I entered the army in 1968 as a private E-1, knowing that if I did everything right, I could be commissioned a second lieutenant in about a year. Then it would be at least another two or three years before I could earn the rank of captain.

But an incredible thing happened in our barracks one day. Three guys walked into the company commander's office as private E-1's, and 15 minutes later walked out as captains. The drill sergeants, who had made their lives miserable only hours before, stood back and saluted. What happened?

Well, those three guys had completed law school before being drafted. The army needed lawyers, so they offered any qualified soldier a direct commission to the rank of captain. The rest of us could only dream about what an instant promotion would be like.

It's the stuff of fairy tales and legends: the genie in the bottle who grants three wishes; the factory worker who inherits a million dollars; the waitress who is "discovered" and becomes a star. In fairy tales, people live "happily ever after." But in real life, they often have problems handling success.

The person with three wishes uses the first two selfishly, and then has to use the third wish to get out of the trouble he's gotten himself into. The instant millionaire finds that his new standard of living cuts him off from family and friends, and he wonders why winning seems so much like losing. The overnight "star" takes her own life at age 29, and no one can understand why a person who "has it all" could ever come to such a tragic end.

Success is a dangerous thing, and instant success is even more threatening. When our circumstances take a dramatic turn for the better, that's the time to be on guard. The dam only breaks when the lake is full.

Free at Last

Maybe you've been wondering if anything good would ever happen to Joseph. After nine chapters

How to Handle Success / 103

of bad news, it *is* refreshing to see him get a couple of breaks. You can imagine how glad *he* must have been. Here is how it happened:

When Pharaoh had a dream that no one could interpret, his cupbearer suddenly remembered a two-year-old promise to a young man in prison. Joseph was summoned before the king where he interpreted Pharaoh's dreams and advised him what to do in light of their meaning. *Poof!* Pharaoh put Joseph in charge of the entire land of Egypt.

What a promotion! Genesis 41:41-45 describes Pharaoh's treatment of Joseph:

• *"Pharaoh took his signet ring from his finger and put it on Joseph's finger"* (v. 42). That ring was Pharaoh's official seal of approval to documents and decrees. Its wearer had great authority and power.

• Pharaoh *"dressed him in robes of fine linen and put a gold chain around his neck"* (v. 42). Clothing has always been a symbol of a person's status in life, and suddenly Joseph had gone from prison rags to designer cloaks.

• *Pharaoh had Joseph "ride in a chariot as his second-in-command, and men shouted before him, 'Make way!'"* (v. 43) Joseph would never again take the bus. From now on, he would travel first class with a police escort. What a feeling of importance and power.

• *Pharaoh also put Joseph "in charge of the whole land of Egypt"* (v. 43). Pharaoh said, "Without your word, no one will lift hand or foot in all Egypt" (v. 44). Joseph was a one-man cabinet in charge of everything from agriculture to the IRS.

• *Pharaoh gave Joseph a wife* (v. 45). The poor

guy hasn't even had a date in over 10 years, and all of a sudden he was married. One day he had no romantic prospects whatsoever, and the next he was standing at the altar. Quite a change!

- *"And Joseph went throughout the land of Egypt"* (v. 45). I wonder how many days Joseph had looked out of Potiphar's window, and later from the prison, and wondered what this new country was like where he was being held? His freedom expanded overnight from the four walls of his cell to the four corners of the Egyptian world. And his whole trip was at government expense.

Joseph's life changed in a dramatic way, but his reaction was even more amazing. His change in fortune *didn't phase him a bit*! He went right on being the same person he had been before —faithful to God and a servant of others. How did Joseph avoid the problems that usually come with instant success?

Whose Credit?

Joseph gave all the credit to God. Pharaoh summoned Joseph from prison and said, in effect: "I understand you can interpret dreams." Joseph simply told him, "I can't, but God can." This was not false modesty, but a genuine desire to give credit where it was due.

I am learning that the best way to accept a compliment is just to say, "Thank you." Every time someone says something nice to me, I don't have to put myself down and give a testimony of what a horrible person I'd be if it weren't for the Lord. But I do have to watch my heart.

Modesty and humility must exist inside me, not just in the words I say. It's easy to mumble, "It's not me, but God," yet secretly be thinking, "I owe it all to God, but He couldn't have done it without me." Joseph's answer to Pharaoh was a natural expression of complete dependence on God.

Ken Medema is a talented musician with the unusual ability to compose and perform his music "off-the-cuff." I once attended a meeting where Ken talked and shared his faith with a group of college students for three hours. To close our time together, the professor in charge asked Ken if he could play and sing something.

Ken sat down at the piano, bowed his head for a moment, then began to play and sing. He summarized our discussion with lyrics and a melody he created as he sang. The music flowed beautifully, the words were meaningful, and all the lines rhymed. Unbelievable! It is even more remarkable because Ken Medema is blind.

Another time Ken performed at the church I attend. As the congregation applauded his performance, Ken stood beside the piano, lifted his sightless eyes heavenward, and began applauding along with the rest of us. Like Joseph, he gave the glory to God.

How Sweet Is Revenge?

Here's a second reason Joseph handled success successfully. *He never used his success to get revenge.* When he was made second-in-command of the country, guess who was now under his authority? Mr. and Mrs. Potiphar, the warden who took credit for Joseph's work, and the forgetful cupbearer, among others. Those four people shared the responsibility for Joseph's years in prison. What would you have done? Made sure that all of them paid for their actions? Made them worry and sweat over how you would eventually get even with them?

Revenge is a common theme in books, music, television, and films. People love to cheer when the hero catches up with the bad guy and beats the tar out of him. We don't have to learn to like revenge. It's a response that comes from deep within our nature.

It is only natural for us to want to get even with people who have wronged us. The greater the wrong, the more vengeful we become. But in God's eyes we don't have a right to seek revenge. Instead, we should follow the same good advice that the Apostle Paul gave to the church in Rome:

> Do not repay anyone evil for evil. Be careful to do what is right in the eyes of everybody. If it is possible, as far as it depends on you, live at peace with everyone. Do not take revenge, my friends, but leave room for God's wrath, for it is written: "It is Mine to avenge; I will repay," says the Lord. On the contrary: "If your enemy is hungry, feed him; if he is thirsty, give him something to drink. In doing this, you will heap burning coals on his head." Do not be overcome by evil, but overcome evil with good
>
> (Romans 12:17-21).

Joseph never used his new authority to punish those who had wronged him. He was content to leave the past behind and let God take care of any injustice.

Success Didn't Change Him

A third reason Joseph's success didn't spoil him is that *he didn't let his promotion change the basic direction of his life.* He viewed this new position as a gift of God, in line with His purposes. Joseph never saw his high status as something he deserved or had earned through all his years of suffering.

The names Joseph gave his two sons are clear indications that he never left the path of faith he had chosen years before.

"Joseph named his firstborn Manasseh and said, 'It is because God has made me forget all my trouble and all my father's household.' The second son he named Ephraim and said, 'It is because God has made me fruitful in the land of my suffering'" (Genesis 41:51-52).

Let's do a little calculating. When we first saw Joseph he was 17 years old. When he entered Pharaoh's service, he was 30. His two sons were born during the seven years of abundance, so by the end of Genesis 41, Joseph must be about 37 years old. Had he changed in the last 20 years?

Yes and no. Sure, Joseph had grown and matured. No doubt he had acquired a great deal of wisdom and experience during that time. But in reality he was still the same person he had always been. His faith was strong and he was still giving himself in service to God and to others.

Years ago I heard someone say that as we grow older, we don't really change; we just become "more so." I'm beginning to realize how true that statement is. Many things about us, including our individual personalities and approaches to life, will probably not change much for the rest of our lives.

A couple of years ago, I went back to my hometown of Oklahoma City for my father's funeral. One day while I was there, I received a phone call from a classmate who had been one of my best friends from sixth grade through high school. I hadn't seen him in over 15 years.

He said, "Well, you probably wouldn't recognize me if you saw me on the street. I have a beard now and most of the hair on my head is gone. I'm a little heavier now too."

But do you know what? I recognized his voice as soon as I answered the phone. He didn't sound a bit different than he ever had. His laugh was the same and he still had the enthusiasm and optimistic outlook on life he had in the sixth grade. Some physical characteristics had changed, but he was still the same.

It made me wonder how much I had changed. It also reminded me that the best way to make the kinds of changes that matter is to remain faithful to God. He is the only One who can do the work inside me that needs to be done.

The greatest change that can happen is to become a new person through faith in Christ. The Bible states clearly: "If anyone is in Christ, he is a new creation; the old has gone, the new has come!" (2 Corinthians 5:17)

Have you made the wonderful discovery of knowing Jesus Christ as your personal Saviour? Have you determined the basic direction of your life by committing yourself to follow Christ without reservation each day? I hope so.

The great paradox of the Christian life is that

we can change only as we refuse to change. Double talk? Not really. As we steadfastly follow Christ, refusing to change our commitment to Him, God changes us from within to make us more like Jesus. "And we, who with unveiled faces all reflect the Lord's glory, are being tranformed into His likeness with ever-increasing glory, which comes from the Lord, who is the Spirit" (2 Corinthians 3:18).

In the middle of suffering and success, Joseph maintained a singleness of heart. God was with him and he with God, both in prison and in the palace. Promotion didn't change Joseph's commitment.

Failing at Success

When is it most difficult to follow Christ? When things are difficult? Or when they are going well? I've found that the easy times are the most dangerous. When the pressure lets up, I want to take a few days off spiritually, to relax and tell myself I've earned a little reward.

The warning sign of Scripture is well-placed which says: "So, if you think you are standing firm, be careful that you don't fall!" (1 Corinthians 10:12)

In the Old Testament we find the accounts of many men who couldn't handle success. Three kings, Solomon, Rehoboam, and Hezekiah, are among those who dropped the ball in the midst of prosperity. When things began going well, they forgot the Lord.

Before the nation of Israel entered the Promised Land, Moses gave them this warning:

When you have eaten and are satisfied, praise the Lord your God for the good land He has given you. Be careful that you do not forget the Lord your God, failing to observe His commands, His laws, and His decrees that I am giving you this day. Otherwise, when you eat and are satisfied, when you build fine houses and settle down, and when your herds and flocks grow large and your silver and gold increase and all you have is multiplied, then your heart will become proud and you will forget the Lord your God, who brought you out of Egypt, out of the land of slavery

(Deuteronomy 8:10-14).

Try Success

When did Joseph achieve success? When he interpreted Pharoh's dream? When he got his new clothes, his chauffeur, his Egyptian Express card, and his wife? That's when he became *prosperous*, but he achieved *success* long before that. In God's eyes, Joseph was always a success.

Remember when Joseph was a servant in Potiphar's house? "The Lord gave him success in everything he did" (Genesis 39:3).

How about all those days in prison? "The Lord was with Joseph and gave him success in whatever he did" (Genesis 39:23).

Prosperity and promotion have ruined a lot of people, even in high school. When someone lets honor and achievement "go to his head," he is headed for a fall.

In his beautiful poem, "If," Rudyard Kipling

wrote as a man giving his son advice for successful living. He included these words: "If you can meet with Triumph and Disaster and treat those two imposters just the same...." Triumph and Disaster are both imposters, but of the two, I think Triumph has brought more grief to the people of God.

Joseph managed to keep his life centered on God in spite of his dramatic change in fortune. Why? Because in the midst of adversity he had learned that success is not money, position, power, pleasure, popularity, or any of the things we so often think it is.

Success is having the presence and power of God in our lives, no matter what the circumstances. God had been with Joseph in Potiphar's house, in prison, and in the palace. No amount of wealth or prosperity could improve that kind of success.

As we see Joseph being promoted to the palace, we might think, *All right! Finally, he has received the reward he deserves.* But the promotion was not Joseph's reward. He had his reward all along—the presence and power of God in his life. Remember what the Lord said to Abraham: "Do not be afraid, Abram. *I* am your shield, your very great reward" (Genesis 15:1, *italics mine*).

We don't need the glitter, the lights, the recognition, or any of the other things so often associated with reward or success. We just need to know that God is with us, and is at work in us and through us to accomplish His purposes.

It has been said that humility is knowing who God is and knowing who we are. Such a perspective enables us to accept promotion and praise while giving God the credit for everything in our lives. It frees us from wanting to reach back into the past for revenge on those who have wronged us. It gives us the ability to enjoy success without changing the basic direction of our lives and our commitment to God.

The keys to handling "success" are knowing what it is, where it comes from, and who to thank for it. Those keys unlock the doorway to humility. The wise choose to walk through it.

Getting Rid of the Garbage
11

Genesis 42—44

A garbage collection company in our city has its motto printed on all its trucks: "Satisfaction guaranteed or double your trash back." The slogan is meant as a joke, but every now and then you read about someone who gives the phrase "garbage collector" a new meaning.

A few years ago, an apartment manager in Detroit let himself into a woman's apartment to check on a water leak. He was astounded to find the entire floor covered by a four-foot layer of empty cans and paper trash. The fire department estimated it to be a seven-year collection of garbage.

The apartment manager couldn't believe it. He described the woman as a model tenant. He said she dressed nicely, never caused trouble, and always paid her rent on time. But no one knew what things were like behind the closed door of her apartment. The place was a mess because, for some unknown reason, she chose to keep her garbage instead of throwing it away.

Forgiveness, in a spiritual sense, is the way we "take out the trash." Forgiveness is the means by which we keep our lives from being filled up with the clutter of everyday living. Forgiveness is a choice—one that we see demonstrated in the life of Joseph.

Dream Come True

In Genesis 42—44, we have the account of Joseph coming face-to-face with his brothers once again. It is the second year of the famine. Joseph is 39 years old, and it has been 22 years since he and his brothers last faced each other. At that time he was down in an empty cistern and they were on top of the situation, deciding whether or not to kill him.

Now things are different. His brothers have come to Egypt to buy grain because there is none in their homeland. The Bible says that Joseph recognized his brothers as soon as he saw them, but "pretended to be a stranger and spoke harshly to them" (Genesis 42:7). Perhaps he disguised his voice and his mannerisms so they wouldn't discover his real identity.

Put yourself in Joseph's place for a minute. Remember the cruelty of your brothers in selling you into slavery. Think of the years working your way up from the bottom at Potiphar's house, the years in prison, and the disappointments when it appeared that you would never again be free.

Now the men who made all that happen are

Getting Rid of the Garbage / 115

standing in front of you. Not only that, but they have bowed down before you. Remember the two dreams you had years ago? In spite of everything and everyone, those dreams have come true. God has fulfilled in your life the things He spoke to you about so long ago.

There is a passage in Psalms with a profound application to this scene:

> The Lord delights in the way of the man
>   whose steps He has made firm;
> though he stumble, he will not fall,
>   for the Lord upholds him with His hand.
> I was young and now I am old,
>   yet I have never seen the righteous
>   forsaken or their children begging bread.
> They are always generous and lend
>   freely; their children will be blessed.
> Turn from evil and do good;
>   then you will always live securely.
> For the Lord loves the just
>   and will not forsake His faithful ones
>   (Psalm 37:23-28).

This passage begins by speaking about the person in whom the Lord delights and has made secure. It goes on to describe some obstacles God helps that person overcome.

Does it remind you of anyone you know? There is a great deal of Joseph's character here, from beginning to end. One significant phrase in this passage is the instruction in verse 27: "Turn from evil and do good." When your dreams come true and God gives you victory over those who have attempted to defeat you, it is never a time for saying "I told you so" or for taking revenge. It's a time to humbly thank the God who made it happen.

Turning the Tables

Put yourself back into Joseph's sandals. The men who have filled your life with hardship and suffering are now bowing down before you. They are under your thumb. You can do anything to them. If you were Joseph, what would *you* do?

• Have their fingernails pulled out?
• Put *them* in jail for 13 years?
• Send them home empty-handed and hope they die on the way?
• Make them apologize and grovel in the sand before you'll even consider their request?

What did Joseph do? Some people feel that Joseph punished his brothers by accusing them of being spies and imprisoning them for three days (Genesis 42:17). People who hold this view say that confining Simeon until the others brought back their youngest brother Benjamin was nothing more than revenge (Genesis 42:20, 24).

But many others see these actions as Joseph's way of finding out if his brothers had changed over the years. Were they still the selfish, hostile group of men he had known in Canaan? If Joseph had wanted revenge, he certainly could have done a better job.

Personally, I believe that Joseph had *forgiven* his brothers long before he ever saw them in Egypt. It may have happened on that long road into captivity, as he worked in Potiphar's house, or in prison. But at some point Joseph had decided in his heart to forgive them, whether or not they would ever ask for forgiveness.

He had forgiven and forgotten what happened on that day long ago, but his brothers were still

Getting Rid of the Garbage / 117

suffering guilt from it. "They said to one another, 'Surely we are being punished because of our brother. We saw how distressed he was when he pleaded with us for his life, but we would not listen; that's why this distress has come upon us.'

"Reuben replied, 'Didn't I tell you not to sin against the boy? But you wouldn't listen! Now we must give an accounting for his blood' " (Genesis 42:21-22).

Imagine that! I wonder how many other problems during the past 22 years they had blamed on their sin against Joseph. Had they been living in constant fear of getting zapped by God?

With Joseph and his brothers, we have a vivid contrast showing what happens when we choose forgiveness, and what happens when we don't. Joseph chose to forgive. His brothers still needed forgiveness, from God and from Joseph.

For the past 22 years:

• *Joseph had been free from guilt.* His brothers were still carrying their guilt.

• *Joseph had forgiven, forgotten, and moved on with life.* His brothers were haunted by what they had done.

• *Joseph had seen God's faithfulness in his life.* His brothers had "seen" the hand of God poised above them, waiting to strike in punishment for their sin.

• *Joseph had been physically imprisoned, but spiritually free.* His brothers had been physically free, but spiritually imprisoned.

If Joseph had not forgiven his brothers, he never would have made it through all his many dark days. If he had been motivated by revenge, he would have destroyed himself from the inside out.

The Enemy Within

Unresolved anger is a cancer. Yet it rarely affects the person toward whom it is directed. The angry, unforgiving person gets ulcers, but the one toward whom the anger is expressed may not even notice.

One of the most dangerous methods of drug smuggling is that of placing small amounts of pure heroin in rubber balloons and swallowing them. The smuggler is able to pass undetected through customs.

Sometimes it works, but if one of the balloons breaks, pure heroin is spilled into the stomach and results in death from overdose.

While drug smuggling is unfamiliar to most of us, we often try to smuggle bitterness and resentment past God's watchful eye. We think they are tightly packaged, but actually the lethal poison of unforgiveness is already eating away at our insides.

A little too dramatic? I wish it were, but it isn't. As Christians, we can either forgive or die spiritually. We can get rid of the garbage in our lives or be poisoned by it. We can enjoy the clean air of God's grace, or live in the polluted atmosphere of unresolved anger and unforgiven sin.

Let's consider two kinds of forgiveness.

God's Forgiveness

First, there is the forgiveness we need to receive from God. In Christ, "we have redemption through His blood, the forgiveness of sins, in accordance

Getting Rid of the Garbage / 119

with the riches of God's grace" (Ephesians 1:7). When we invite Jesus Christ to be our Lord and Saviour, our sins are forgiven and we become children of God. We are no longer His enemies, but His friends. Yet we still have the old sinful nature within us, and we find ourselves sinning. What then?

"If we confess our sins, He is faithful and just and will forgive us our sins and purify us from all unrighteousness" (1 John 1:9). This verse has been called "the Christian's bar of soap." It is our provision for daily cleansing, and we should claim it as soon as we become aware of a sin in our lives.

But sometimes sins dirty up our lives, and we don't take care of them when we should. Time passes and we know that things aren't right between us and the Lord. Yet the longer we hide our sins, the more difficult it becomes to do something about them.

Five words can help clean out the garbage in our lives:

(1) *Conviction*—This is the work God does in us as He makes us aware of our sin. Jesus described this work of the Holy Spirit by saying: "When He comes, He will convict the world of guilt in regard to sin and righteousness and judgment" (John 16:8).

Conviction may be a tiny prick of conscience or a crushing awareness of how we have failed God or wronged another person. Either way, it is God's voice calling us to receive His forgiveness. God doesn't nag, but He does convict so that we will come to Him.

(2) *Confession*—This is the act of simply admitting our sins to God. Confession is telling the Lord exactly what we've done wrong, then asking for forgiveness.

The most important part of confession is the attitude of our hearts. It's easy to get into the habit of saying certain phrases without really meaning them. God sees our hearts. He knows when we mean what we are praying, and when we are only mouthing empty words.

(3) *Forgiveness*—This is God's work. He has promised to forgive us on the basis of Christ's shed blood. Jesus paid the penalty for our sins, and His death satisfied the justice and righteousness of God. On that basis, God forgives our sins.

It's important to remember that God doesn't forgive us because we deserve it, feel terrible inside, or promise to try harder. He forgives because Christ has already paid the penalty for our sin. God also forgives with a completeness that we find humanly impossible to understand.

"As far as the east is from the west, so far has He removed our transgressions from us" (Psalm 103:12). That's a picture of infinity. How far is the east from the west? You can only go north or south on this planet for about 12,500 miles. Then you reach a pole and start going the opposite direction.

But if you start going east, you could go east forever. East is an infinite distance from west, and that's how far God has removed our sins from us.

(4) *Restitution*—This is something *we* should do. Our sin often affects someone else. Restitution is the action we take to make things right with those we have wronged. It may be an apology for something we said. It might involve returning something which we have stolen, or paying for something which we have damaged or destroyed.

It is not a requirement to being forgiven by God,

Getting Rid of the Garbage / 121

but it is an important part of the God-given process for dealing with sin.

Remember what happened to Zaccheus, the dishonest tax collector, when he met Jesus? "But Zaccheus stood up and said to the Lord, 'Look Lord! Here and now I give half my possessions to the poor, and if I have cheated anybody out of anything, I will pay back four times the amount'" (Luke 19:8).

I have had to do some painful things during my life in order to make restitution to those I have wronged. But let me tell you, it is a wonderful feeling to know that the garbage is cleaned out and things are right with people around me.

(5) *Resolution*—This is something that God does by giving us His peace and an assurance that our sin problem has been settled. This assurance comes from God and does not depend on anyone else's response.

I went into a bus station one day to make a phone call and found that I had no change. There was no one near the cash register, so I walked behind the lunch counter to ask a lady in the back room if she could help me.

She chewed me out for coming behind the lunch counter, and I retaliated with a few choice words of my own about her need to pay attention to what was going on. I knew my reaction was wrong, so a few minutes later I walked back to the counter and apologized to the woman.

I told her I was a Christian, that my harsh words had been wrong, and that I hoped she would accept my apology. She wouldn't. Instead she let go with another verbal blast about how I should never have come behind the counter.

I apologized again for my actions and my words, and left. As far as I was concerned, the issue had been resolved. I was completely at peace even though the lady had chosen to cling to her anger.

It helps to know that we have been understood and forgiven by those we wrong, but some people will be unable or unwilling to forgive. Even in those cases, we can be at peace and know that in our hearts the issue has been resolved.

The bus station incident helped me understand how the Lord works in our lives to clear the clutter. God *convicted* me about my words. I *confessed* my sin to Him. He *forgave* me. I made *restitution* through an apology to the woman I had wronged and the issue for me, was *resolved*. That's God's plan for us when it comes to dealing with sin, past or present, in our lives.

Man's Forgiveness

The second type of forgiveness is the kind we need to extend to others.

"Get rid of all bitterness, rage and anger, brawling and slander, along with every form of malice. Be kind and compassionate to one another, forgiving each other, just as in Christ God forgave you" (Ephesians 4:31-32).

Has someone done something to you which you feel you will never be able to forgive? Are you holding a grudge against another person, waiting for the time you can get back at him? It may be a parent, brother, sister, or relative who has wronged you. It could be a teacher who was unfair in grading or discipline. Perhaps it's a former

Getting Rid of the Garbage / 123

employer who fired you on the basis of false information, or a friend that deserted you when you needed him most.

Maybe the facts prove you are right and the other person is wrong, but still you are mistreated. When unfair treatment causes bitterness inside you, *you* are the only one who can get rid of it—by choosing to forgive.

You can forgive that other person even if he never recognizes his guilt and asks your forgiveness. In doing so, you'll take the only step that can free you to enjoy your future in spite of what may have happened in the past.

We should forgive others *because God has forgiven us.* But often, childish attitudes get in the way. Did you ever give a small child a toy and ask him to let all his friends play with it? Good luck. Little kids are often hesitant to share something new with those around them.

But children aren't the only ones with that problem. God has been so generous with His forgiveness given to us in Christ. He offers it freely to us, saying, "Share it with each other, will you?"

One of the most sobering stories Jesus told was of the servant who had been forgiven a huge debt by his master. But that same servant imprisoned another servant who could not pay him a small amount. When the master heard of it, he sent the unforgiving servant to jail until he paid all he owed. Then Jesus said: "This is how My heavenly Father will treat each of you unless you forgive your brother from your heart" (Matthew 18:35).

We are to forgive in the same way that God has forgiven us. Think of how God forgives: freely, completely, joyfully, with no strings attached.

Better Medicine

A popular antacid claims to consume 47 times its own weight in excess stomach acid. Another product gives a visual demonstration of its ability to neutralize all those terrible juices that produce heartburn. Every year we spend millions to relieve the pain of what we eat and what's eating us.

But Christians should spell relief, "F-O-R-G-I-V-E-N-E-S-S." Real inner peace is the result of God's forgiveness—that which we receive for ourselves and that which we give to others. It's a matter of regularly taking out our inner garbage and making sure that our spiritual lives remain clean.

When was the last time you cleaned out your locker? Your desk? Your room? Your closet? Your heart?

> Search me, O God, and know my heart;
> test me and know my anxious thoughts.
> See if there is any offensive way in me,
> and lead me in the way everlasting
> (Psalm 139:23-24).

Joseph made the choice to forgive a group of men who had done everything they could to ruin his life. Long before he and his brothers faced each other in Egypt, he had settled the issue with God. Joseph was free because he chose to forgive.

Why, God?

12

Genesis 45:1-28

I was involved in taping a television project in Las Vegas. One scene was scheduled to be shot in front of the fountains at a well-known hotel. But we had a problem—it was January, so the fountains weren't on.

Our producer inquired about using them briefly for our taping, and was told that the person to see was the doorman. After a brief conversation and a $20 tip, the fountains came to life—on a crisp winter day, exactly when we needed them. When it came to those fountains, the doorman was in charge. He had *sovereignty*. *Sovereignty* is "supremacy of authority or rule; royal rank, authority, or power; complete independence and self-government" (*American Heritage Dictionary*). In everyday language, someone who is *sovereign* can do whatever he wants any time and any way he pleases.

Power Plus

When we associate sovereignty with people, we see it misused for selfish reasons and limited in its power. But the sovereignty of God is neither limited nor misused. He has the power to act in any way He chooses throughout the universe. But He exercises His complete authority in a much different way than His human creations.

History shows that power corrupts. Rulers and kings have often brought about their own downfalls because they couldn't handle power. Very few people with political clout, wealth, or great influence have used their power for the good of others. Not so with our heavenly Father.

In His sovereignty, God is at work in our lives for our good and His glory. We often don't understand His sovereignty. And at times God seems to have gone on vacation or forgotten about us. But the Lord who loves us is aware of every detail of our lives. He is at work to bring all those details together for good.

We need to remember two things about the absolute power and authority of God:

(1) *God's sovereign acts are always based on what He knows, which is far beyond what we know.*

For My thoughts are not your thoughts, neither are your ways My ways," declares the Lord. "As the heavens are higher than the earth, so are My ways higher than your ways and My thoughts than your thoughts

(Isaiah 55:8-9).

Scientists are planning to place an orbiting telescope aboard the U.S. space shuttle. The telescope will operate outside the haze of the earth's atmosphere, so astronomers expect to see farther into space than ever before. The telescope will give them a new perspective.

In these days of rapid technological change, this news hardly phases us. Yet it has only been a few years since we discovered what our own planet looks like from outer space. On August 7, 1959 Explorer VI, an unmanned U.S. satellite, transmitted the first picture of Earth from space. It gave man his first likeness of this planet based on something more than projections and conjectures.

Today we accept the idea of a space perspective without blinking an eye. Royal weddings and international sports events are brought to us by satellite. We monitor the activities of volcanoes, nuclear tests, and tropical storms from our eyes in the sky, and never question the fact that they have a better perspective on the world than we have.

But we have a hard time giving God the same trust we give a satellite. We aren't sure that God knows the best way to direct our lives. When disappointments and delays come our way, we wonder why God would let those things happen to us.

The fact is we will probably never know the "why" of many difficult things that come into our lives. People we love may die long before we think they should. The divorce of our parents may leave us feeling alone and rejected just when we need love and security the most. Disability or injury may end many of our dreams before they have really begun. We may desperately want to know "why?" But a more important question is "who?"

God is not the source of our tragedy and pain,

but He can and does use them in our lives. From His perspective, He can see how these "detours" of life will take us around certain dangers and obstacles, and move us toward the goals He has planned for us.

When it seems that things are out of control or that God is not taking any calls, remember that His sovereign acts are always based on what He knows.

(2) *God's sovereignty is firmly rooted in His love for us.* Because of that, we can move through fear into faith, even during trying times.

> If anyone acknowledges that Jesus is the Son of God, God lives in him and he in God. And so we know and rely on the love God has for us. God is love. Whoever lives in love lives in God, and God in him. Love is made complete among us so that we will have confidence on the day of judgment, because in this world we are like Him. There is no fear in love. But perfect love drives out fear, because fear has to do with punishment. The man who fears is not made perfect in love
>
> (1 John 4:15-18).

There is an old movie called *Jason And the Argonauts*. The plot is based on Greek mythology, and throughout the film, the scene returns to the top of Mt. Olympus, the home of the gods. Zeus and his wife Hera are sitting next to a table whose surface resembles the ocean. On it are miniature ships, monsters, and figures representing men.

In this cosmic game of chess, Zeus gets a move and then Hera gets one. The people involved are simply pawns in the hands of the gods. They are manipulated because of the curiosity and selfish motives of the deities who rule them.

Is that how God deals with us? Hardly. All of God's actions toward us are motivated by His love. But sometimes it's hard to see God's loving hand when we face sufferings or tragedy. During those times only faith in what the Bible says about God will carry us through.

God, I Don't Understand

Not long ago, a friend of mine lost his 21-year-old son. The young man had been a star athlete and an outspoken witness for Christ on his college campus. When his heart failed after open-heart surgery, his death came as a crushing blow to everyone who knew him.

After the funeral, my friend and his wife sent a letter to many people who had prayed for their son and for the family. In closing, the letter read, "We're trying to discover why God has chosen to show His love to us in this way." In the midst of their terrible pain, faith was still there, reaching out to embrace a loving Father and say, "I don't understand, but I still believe."

In Genesis 45, we find Joseph unable to control his emotions any longer, and in an outburst of tears he reveals his identity to his brothers. As you might expect, they are speechless with terror.

"This is it," they must have been thinking. "We ruined Joseph's life years ago, and now things have come full circle back on our own heads. Will he kill us quickly or make us suffer?"

Joseph had already demonstrated some model attitudes and actions, but his statement to his brothers has to rank right up there with his best:

"I am your brother Joseph, the one you sold into Egypt! And now, do not be distressed and do not be angry with yourselves for selling me here, because it was to save lives that God sent me ahead of you. For two years now there has been famine in the land, and for the next five years there will not be plowing and reaping. But God sent me ahead of you to preserve for you a remnant on earth and to save your lives by a great deliverance. So then, it was not you who sent me here, but God" (Genesis 45:4-8).

Three times Joseph said it: "God sent me ahead of you," "God sent me," and "it was not you who sent me here, but God."

Twenty-two years after being dragged out of a dry well and sold as a slave, Joseph faced the men who did it. And he accepted the sovereignty of God in all of their lives. I don't know about you, but that causes me to ask myself some questions.

Getting Even

How do I respond to people who do hateful things to me? My first reaction may be one of revenge. I may hurt them back without thinking about it. But what do I do when God quietly speaks to me and points out my wrong attitude? Am I willing to apologize and seek forgiveness, even though another's wrong action contributed to my sin?

Remember, Joseph wasn't facing people who had simply made fun of the way he looked or who put Limburger cheese in his locker. These guys had set out to kill him. But because he was worth more alive, they decided to just ruin his life.

God had overruled their plans and had actually used their destructive actions as part of His plan to save them all. It was all clear to Joseph now, but he would never have seen things in that light if he had refused to trust in the sovereignty of God.

Bail Out

Joseph's positive attitude raises another question in my mind: *How convinced am I of God's sovereignty?* Is it something that I only agree to intellectually, or do I believe in it enough to carry me through the storms of life? Am I really convinced that God is in control of my life?

Remember when Jesus and His disciples were crossing the Sea of Galilee and a terrific storm came up? (Mark 4:35-41) The wind was screaming and the waves were crashing over the sides of the boat. The water was coming in faster than the disciples could bail it out, and they panicked.

Think about the situation for a minute. How many of those disciples were fishermen by trade? At least four that we know of: Simon Peter, his brother Andrew, and James and John, the sons of Zebedee. Surely these four had been caught in numerous storms on the Sea of Galilee, and were well qualified to judge the danger they were in. So if these four thought they were going to sink, how do you suppose the rest of the disciples felt?

And what was Jesus doing? He was in the back of the boat, asleep.

"Don't you care if we drown?" the disciples asked as they woke Jesus up (Mark 4:38). "Our life is about to end. This storm is more than we can handle. Aren't You going to do anything? Don't You know? Don't You care?"

Jesus calmly stopped the storm then asked them, "Why are you so afraid? Do you still have no faith?" (Mark 4:40) On other occasions, Jesus would ask them, "Don't you know Me ... even after I have been among you such a long time?" (John 14:9)

We must face the same question. It is possible to spend a lifetime going to church without coming to know Jesus Christ in a personal, life-changing way. We can know all the right words to say, yet have no real faith in our hearts toward God.

Double Standard

When I was a ninth-grader, a girl from our school came to visit our youth group. Someone asked me to lead in prayer, which I did. Later the girl told me, "That was a beautiful prayer."

I thanked her for the compliment, but inwardly thought, "If you knew how I acted the rest of the week, you wouldn't think it was so great." I had one vocabulary and set of actions for my parents and the people at church, and another for my friends at school. I knew the "right" language, but I had never really given my life to Christ and started living for Him.

It is also possible to be a Christian, yet never choose to trust God's sovereignty. Instead we can manipulate to get our way and fight those who try to stop us.

It is significant to note that when Joseph told his

brothers, "God has sent me here," he immediately went on to include *them* in God's plan. I might be tempted to tell them how God had provided for *me*, give them a little grain just to show how generous I was, and send them on their way.

Joseph said, "I want you and your families to move to Egypt with me. I'm just a part of God's plan to save us all." When we choose to trust God's sovereignty, we acknowledge that He can deal as He pleases with the people who have wronged us. He doesn't have to rain fire and brimstone on them. He can forgive them and include them in His love and care, just as He does us.

When God tells us to leave vengeance in His hands (Romans 12:19), there is always the option that people will repent and avoid His wrath. But if we serve God faithfully, we often have a hard time living with His grace toward those who wander away and come back.

In the Parable of the Prodigal Son, the older brother overlooked his younger brother's repentance and his father's forgiveness. He cared nothing about restoring a family relationship. All he could do was gripe because his father had never thrown a party for him (Luke 15:11-32).

Jonah complained because the people of Nineveh repented and God spared them. He was disappointed and angry as he sat on the hillside, waiting for the big sinner-scorching fireball that never came (Jonah 3:10—4:3).

Joseph was willing to be an instrument in God's hands to help the people who had hated him. He was willing to trust his all-powerful God to make the right decision, even if it included grace and goodness for his former enemies.

Master Plan

When I think about Joseph's response, a final question comes to mind: *Am I willing to trust God's sovereignty through all the dark days when He seems to be doing nothing to change my difficult circumstances?*

God never forces anyone to be part of His plan. Joseph could have chosen not to cooperate. But his daily decisions through the years of serving and imprisonment kept him *available* to God.

God is sovereign, but He doesn't manipulate people like pawns. He never forces us to follow His way. We always have a choice about our attitudes and actions.

God's overall purposes are never defeated by our lack of cooperation. If we choose to turn our backs on Him, He will find someone else to do the job. We may ruin our own lives by rebelling against the Lord, but we won't prevent His work in the world.

Have you ever gotten mad at a tree or a wall and kicked it? Who lost in that little encounter? That's the way it is when we get mad at God and go our own way. All we succeed in doing is injuring ourselves. God is grieved by our sin, but He is not thrown off course in His purposes and work.

When we acknowledge God's sovereignty, we agree to let Him use everything in our lives to honor Him and to produce goodness and maturity in us.

There are a lot of "whys" in our lives.
- Why am I short instead of tall?
- Why do I have one parent instead of two?

• Why didn't I get accepted by the college I wanted to attend?
• Why can't I find that special person to date and enjoy being with?

We long to know the reasons for the situations that seem difficult and unfair. Yet in the midst of all the "whys," there is another question we must answer: "Who?"

• Who created me the way I am?
• Who has promised to be with me always?
• Who will never leave or forsake me?
• Who will love, protect, and provide for me even if my earthly family should be broken by death or divorce?
• Who is the One who can enable me to love those who hate me?
• Who is with me when everyone else is gone and loneliness is overwhelming?

Joseph discovered that *God* was with him, and that He was working all the time to accomplish His purposes. The God who sees things from a different perspective and bases His actions on His great love was with Joseph all along.

Because he chose to trust God's sovereignty, Joseph could love the men who tried to ruin his life and say to them: "It was not you who sent me here, but God."

Turning Trash into Treasure
13

Genesis 50:15-21

For centuries, people have sought a way to make gold and silver from metals of lesser value. The process is known as *alchemy*—a strange mixture of science, magic, and religion. Alchemists have yet to achieve their goal, but their search still intrigues us. Who wouldn't like to discover a way to convert worthless metal into gold?

What if you could turn trash into treasure, or transform old math papers into $20 bills? You could purchase the local junkyard and turn it into Ft. Knox!

The Alchemy of God

In Joseph's life, we see a process at work which I like to think of as "the alchemy of God." God took his brothers' evil actions and brought good out of them. When their father Jacob died, Joseph's brothers became worried about what Joseph might do to them. They still believed he would take revenge on them. Perhaps he had just been waiting till their father died.

They begged Joseph's forgiveness again, threw themselves down before him, and said, "We are your slaves" (Genesis 50:18).

"But Joseph said to them, 'Don't be afraid. Am I in the place of God? You intended to harm me, but God intended it for good to accomplish what is now being done, the saving of many lives. So then, don't be afraid. I will provide for you and your children.' And he reassured them and spoke kindly to them" (Genesis 50:19-21).

Joseph had experienced the alchemy of God. *"You intended to harm me, but God intended it for good."*

This May Hurt a Little

There are several things which we should notice about "the alchemy of God."

First, *it doesn't keep bad things from happening.* God could have kept Joseph from being sold into slavery, but He didn't. The cruel action planned by Joseph's brothers happened, and it hurt. The result was years of hardship and suffering for Joseph.

I have no idea why God sometimes spares us from suffering and at other times allows it in our lives. I must conclude by faith that He knows what He is doing, and that He remains trustworthy, even when I can't understand His ways.

In this life we may never understand some of God's purposes in our sufferings. "Why?" will remain the great unanswered question.

Bad to Good

The alchemy of God is the process by which God takes the bad events of our lives and causes good to come out of them. It is not some kind of mystical, magical event. It is a *process* clearly outlined in Scripture, stated plainly so that we may understand and accept it.

The alchemy of God doesn't happen overnight. It takes time. Think back to a passage we considered in chapter 7:

"And we rejoice in the hope of the glory of God. Not only so, but we also rejoice in our sufferings, because we know that suffering produces perseverance; perseverance, character; and character, hope. And hope does not disappoint us, because God has poured out His love into our hearts by the Holy Spirit, whom He has given us" (Romans 5:2-5).

Most of us would label suffering "bad" and hope "good." The alchemy of God transforms the common element of suffering into the precious gold of hope, but remember the *process*:
Suffering→Perseverance→Character→Hope

Notice two more references to gold in the following passages: "In this you greatly rejoice, though now for a little while you may have to suffer grief in all kind of trials. These have come so that your faith—of greater worth than gold, which perishes even though refined by fire—may be proved genuine and may result in praise, glory, and honor when Jesus Christ is revealed" (1 Peter 1:6-7).

"But He knows the way that I take; when He has tested me, I will come forth as gold. My feet have closely followed His steps; I have kept to His way without turning aside. I have not departed from the commands of His lips; I have treasured the words of His mouth more than my daily bread" (Job 23:10-12).

When we go to the doctor or dentist, he will usually explain a painful procedure before beginning it. The caring physician tells us what he is going to do and why. He may say, "This is going to hurt," but he goes right ahead with the process.

Jesus has often been called the Great Physician, and as He works in our lives there are some operations that are going to hurt. Understanding God's alchemy can prepare us for those times, so we won't remove ourselves from the process because of the pain.

Sweet Pain

Evangelist Leighton Ford tells the story of a black teenager in Atlanta who endured jeers and threats during the early days of integration in the late 1960s. When he was asked how he felt about his suffering, he said it was "sweet pain," because he knew it was necessary to accomplish something that had to be done.

Psychiatrist Robert Coles picked up on the concept of "sweet pain" and defines it as "the kind of self-sacrifice that comes when one is going through turmoil and stress for a purpose." Dr. Coles even says that "sweet pain" is good for the human spirit. Without it, we learn nothing.

Would you say that Joseph experienced "sweet pain"? How about you? Even though you can't see how your difficult circumstances will be resolved, you can believe God will use them to accomplish His purposes. "We know that in all things God works for the good of those who love Him, who have been called according to His purpose" (Romans 8:28).

Beyond Ourselves

The alchemy of God results in good for others, not just personal happiness for ourselves.

"You intended to harm me," said Joseph, "but God intended it for good to accomplish what is now being done, the saving of many lives" (Genesis 50:20).

It is not just wishful thinking to say that when we submit to God's sovereignty and commit our disappointments and tragedies to Him, He will bring good from them—to us and to others.

Consider how many people were saved from starvation because of Joseph's foresight and management in Egypt. The good which God brought from Joseph's suffering went far beyond his personal happiness and well-being. Joseph could have bailed out of his painful ordeal at any time. But he chose to remain faithful to God and trust Him for the outcome. If we are to experience the alchemy of God in our lives, we will also have to choose to see beyond the present.

One Man's Trash

In 1979, America's Skylab satellite crashed to earth, scattering tons of debris across the desert of western Australia. A lot of protest was heard from "down under" about our litter falling from space, but one man used Skylab's crash as a golden opportunity.

Mervyn Cole decided to turn the space junk into treasure. He collected several large chunks of the fallen spacecraft, and his company produced 10,000 medallions commemorating Skylab's fiery return to earth.

Each medallion contained a piece of Skylab's water tank as a momento. The price? The silver medallions sold for $350 each. The gold ones went for $1,650! Some people see junk where others see treasure. It's all a matter of attitude.

A 72-year-old lady in Los Angeles is known to many as "the Picasso of the junk pile." She creates art from what others throw away. The area around her home is filled with statues, furniture, toys, and items of interest which she has made from trash. Local garbage collectors, neighborhood residents, and friends bring things to her just to see what she will make from them. Her motto is: "I never throw anything away."

God never throws anything or anyone away. There is not an experience of our lives, past or present, that He can't use in His process of bringing good out of bad. We only need to let Him use those experiences. In prayer, we can name the bad, ask Him to take the intentional evil of others or the random tragedies of life, and use them for good.

The alchemy of God turned the "worthless" events of Joseph's life into gold. He can do the same for you.

You Choose

As we have studied the life of Joseph, the issue of *choice* has kept coming up. We have seen:
- *No matter what the situation, you always have a choice.*
- *Your choice always makes a difference.*
- *The ultimate human freedom is to choose your attitude in any given situation.*
- *Your attitude can change any situation.*

We cannot choose our parents, our brothers and sisters, our family background, our nationality, home, school, teachers, size, looks, or intelligence. In many situations it appears that we are powerless to change the course of events.

Yet in every case we can choose two things—our *attitudes* and our *actions*.

You didn't ask for your parents, but you can decide what you think of them and how you will treat them on a daily basis.

No one consulted you when your family was being planned, but you can decide how you will live with the brothers and sisters in your home.

You do have a choice. In the film *Whose Life Is It Anyway?* Richard Dreyfuss played the part of a young artist who was paralyzed from the neck down in an automobile accident. The doctors told him he would never paint or sculpt again. He would never leave his bed under his own power. Marriage was out of the question.

With that future before him, the young man decided he no longer wanted to live. Death appeared the best option. The rest of the film detailed his fight to force the doctors to let him die.

I can't help contrasting that fictional situation with the true story of Joni Eareckson Tada. I mentioned her in chapter 4, but her story is worth repeating. At 17 she was paralyzed from the neck down in a diving accident, and faced a helpless existence as a quadriplegic. She was told she would never feed herself, never drive a car, never marry. She also wanted to die, and would have committed suicide if she had been able. But eventually she chose to follow Christ and to let God's alchemy bring joy to her life. Her story has been an inspiration to thousands of people around the world.

God never "healed" Joni in the traditional sense of the word, but she now paints by holding a brush in her teeth, speaks to audiences across the country, drives a specially equipped van on the California freeways, and is married. What could have been the end of her life was only a new beginning.

What about you? You may have had a beautiful home and every advantage in life up to this point. Or perhaps your family has always had to struggle financially. You may have a physical handicap, or difficulty learning in school. All of our lives are less than perfect.

One thing is for sure: From this point on, the past is merely the introduction to the rest of your life. You must begin taking responsibility for the person you are becoming. You are the only one who can choose for *you* to become what God wants you to be.

Happy Ending?

I have a sister who is in the habit of giving me strange birthday and Christmas presents. They have ranged from a foam rubber snake on a wire leash to a chrome-plated siren whistle.

One year she gave me a hardback book with 150 pages in it—all blank. The accompanying brochure said that everyone has always wanted to write a book, so this was my chance. The only thing that would ever be in that book was what I wrote there.

Life is like that blank book. It has been given to you by God. The introduction has already been written by someone else, but the rest of the book has yet to be composed. The plot is up to you.

Every choice you make is a word in the book. Your attitudes and actions will combine to form the sentences. Before you know it, your habits and character will create paragraphs which quickly grow into pages and chapters.

You can write a tragedy *by* yourself and *for* yourself, or you can join forces with the Lord Jesus Christ, who loved you and gave Himself for you. He wants to help you write an exciting story with a satisfying ending. Which book will you write?

The choice is yours. You are free to choose.